The
Spirit
Of the Gospel

The
Spirit
Of the Gospel

WATCHMAN NEE

Translated from the Chinese

Christian Fellowship Publishers, Inc.
New York

ISBN 0-935008-67-5

Available from the Publishers at:

11515 Allecingie Parkway
Richmond, Virginia 23235

PRINTED IN U.S.A.

TRANSLATOR'S PREFACE

The coming of the Lord Jesus to earth was the casting upon the earth of the fire of the gospel (cf. Luke 12.49). He began with the callings of the twelve and of the seventy to preach the gospel. After He had accomplished the work of redemption by His death, He then commissioned His disciples to preach the gospel throughout the world.

In the recovery of the church the ministry of the gospel must be recovered too. The fire of the gospel must be burning in the church. It is the spirit of the gospel that sends the gospel out with power. The love of God for sinners, the compassions of Christ towards the lost need to fill the hearts of the gospelers.

In this present volume Watchman Nee shares with his younger colleagues the absolute necessity for the spirit of the gospel. He illustrates this with episodes from the life of James M'Kendrick whose spirit of the gospel ran high. Then he gives some practical instructions on how to preach the gospel, such as presenting the Lord Jesus as the Friend of sinners as well as their Savior, helping sinners to get in touch with Jesus Christ, and the four indispensable factors to an acceptance of the gospel. Finally, he touches upon a number of topics which show forth the unsearchable riches of the gospel.

May God use this volume to stir up the spirit of the gospel in the hearts of His people that the fire may spread far and wide upon the earth to the glory of God.

CONTENTS

Translator's Preface   v

Part I   The Spirit of the Gospel   1

Part II   How to Preach the Gospel   17

Part III   The Unsearchable Riches
             of the Gospel   53

    A. God Seeks Men   53

    B. Who Crucified the Lord?   55

    C. Our Lord Always Ministers   61

    D. Present the Bodies   66

    E. Trust and Obey   69

    F. Let the Word of Christ Dwell
        in You Richly   82

    G. Wondrous Things Are Naturally Done   93

Part I and Part II are two lengthy messages on the gospel given by the author at the last training session for workers that was held at Mt. Kuling, near Foochow, China, in 1949. Part III comprises different messages which were given at various times throughout the many years of his faithful ministry. These have now been combined into one volume for the benefit of the readers.

Scripture quotations are from the
American Standard Version of the Bible
(1901), unless otherwise indicated.

Part I

The Spirit of the Gospel

[Jesus said,] I came to cast fire upon the earth; and what do I desire, if it is already kindled? But I have a baptism to be baptized with; and how am I straitened till it be accomplished! Think ye that I am come to give peace in the earth? I tell you, Nay; but rather division: for there shall be from henceforth five in one house divided, three against two, and two against three. They shall be divided, father against son, and son against father; mother against daughter, and daughter against her mother; mother in law against her daughter in law, and daughter in law against her mother in law. (Luke 12.49-53)

Jesus said, Verily I say unto you, There is no man that hath left house, or brethren, or sisters, or mother, or father, or children, or lands, for my sake, and for the gospel's sake, but he shall receive a hundredfold now in this time, houses, and brethren, and sisters, and mothers, and children, and lands, with persecution; and in the world to come eternal life. (Mark 10. 29-30)

Whosoever would save his life shall lose it; and

whosoever shall lose his life for my sake and the gospel's shall save it. (Mark 8. 35)

One

The Lord came to cast fire upon the earth. This fire was kindled in heaven, and it will burn upon the earth. As this fire burns on earth, there will be division, for as Jesus declared, a family of five will be divided into a struggle of two against three. According to Luke 12. 49–53, this fire is cast upon the earth for the sake of the Lord and for the sake of the gospel. As a matter of fact, this fire is the Lord himself and is also the gospel. What is for the sake of the Lord is for the sake of the gospel, and vice versa. The man who in Mark 10 is said to leave all and consecrate all does so also for the Lord's and the gospel's sake. This love burns in God's heart, and it burns in the heart of the Lord Jesus. It burns continuously in the Holy Spirit and is also to burn in the church.

The coming of the Lord Jesus to earth is the casting of the fire of the gospel. He begins with the callings of the twelve and of the seventy to preach the gospel. After He has accomplished the work of redemption by His death, He then commissions His disciples to preach the gospel throughout the world.

With the coming of the Holy Spirit, the church was born and was commissioned to preach the gospel. It is instructive that the four canonical Gospels are placed in the New Testament before the Acts of the Apostles, for the words of the apostles are based on the Gospels.

These men not only preach the truth of the gospel but also propagate the spirit of the gospel. Ever since sin entered the world, it has caused great pain to God as well as insurmountable difficulty to men. Even before men were conscious of their being lost, God had sensed the loss of children. With the burden pressed upon His heart, He designed to deliver men out of hell. Because of this love, God sacrificed His only begotten Son in order to gain many sons in us (cf. Heb. 2. 10). This fire of love was in Christ. It compelled Him to travel a far distance to this earth to save sinners. This fire of love burned in Him, driving Him to the cross to die for sinners. "Many waters cannot quench love, neither can floods drown it" (S.S. 8. 7a). Such love shakes heaven and earth. All who are consumed by this love cannot but cry out, "Woe is unto me if I preach not the gospel" (1 Cor. 9. 16b). This fire burned in the apostles enabling them to die by the sword and by being boiled in caldrons of hot oil.

The mark of being filled with the Holy Spirit is defined in one place in Scripture as the act of getting drunk (see Eph. 5. 18). Having been saved by the Lord, we cannot but lose our usual cool. The recovery of the church is the recovery of the entire range of God's word. Hence the ministry of the gospel must be recovered. The fire of the gospel must be burning in the church and the gospel must be preached to the ends of the earth before our Lord will return (see Matt. 24. 14). That the fire fails to spread abroad is a basic problem. It is because the outward man is not broken. The outward man must be broken; otherwise the gospel will not be able to spread. For the nature of the outward man is opposite to that of the fire. Paul wept for the sake of the gospel. And so did the psalmist of an earlier day: "They that sow in tears shall reap in joy. He that goeth forth and weepeth, bearing seed for sowing, shall doubtless come again with joy, bringing his sheaves with him" (Ps. 126. 5-6).

A need to be gentle, a need to be zealous. The fire should not be suppressed. There is not much fire in the first place. It will die out if it is suppressed. In preaching the gospel, the spirit of the cross and the spirit of the throne must be present in the meeting.

Not simply a preaching, but a kindling. The fire needs to be cast forth from us. We must not think of ourselves. We cannot be lazy. We must weep and cry for the sinners. Our Lord wept over Jerusalem: and such is the spirit of the gospel. The Holy Spirit is the Spirit of Christ, and the Spirit of Christ is the Spirit of the cross. In preaching the gospel of the cross, our whole being is to be the channel by which the fire comes forth.

Two

James M'Kendrick, born in 1859, was a young Scottish coal miner, quite simple and ordinary. But the love of God was set afire in him and destroyed his outward man. He became a broken person; therefore the Lord was able to use him. He got saved when he was twenty-two years of age. Let us listen to what he reported of himself after his conversion:

> On the evening of my conversion, accompanied by an uncle—one of the finest Christian men I have ever known, and one to whom I owe much—I had

occasion to pass a place where my companions were gathered. Immediately I saw them, I said to my uncle, "I must tell my companions that I'm saved." I called the ring-leader aside, and began to tell him how the Lord had saved me that afternoon, and as I did, tears of joy and peace ran down my face. I felt greatly helped and strengthened as I related to him all the experiences of that afternoon, and ere I had finished the tears were running down my companion's face as well. He was deeply impressed with all I said, and rejoining the others, he related to them as best he could what I had told him of my new experience. *

Hence, in the first day of his salvation, his spirit broke out of his outward man.

One evening, wrote M'Kendrick,

I was standing close up against the missionary, with my soul on fire for the salvation of the people. The missionary preached in the usual orthodox fashion, with four or five heads to his discourse, as well as several other stages before he reached the finish. I had little sympathy with his style of preaching, and was longing for him to make a direct personal appeal to the people and beseech them to be saved. I cannot remember what his text was, or what he said, though no doubt it was all sound and good, for he was a good man. But to me it all seemed wide of the mark, and my patience became exhausted, so I gave his coat sleeve a gentle pull. Still he continued preaching, as far from the point as ever. I pulled his coat sleeve a second time more forcibly. He paused, and stooping down, for he was a tall man, he whispered, "What is it?" I said, "Man, stop

*James M'Kendrick, *Seen and Heard during Forty-Six Years' Evangelistic Labours* (London: Pickering & Inglis, [1933]), 28.

and let me speak." He only spoke a few words more, and then said, "James M'Kendrick will now address you."

Immediately he said that, my mind seemed clean swept and garnished. I was speechless, and could not find a word to say, I could not even say "Dear Friends." Yet my soul was on fire for their salvation. My first relief was a flood of tears, not words. At length I cried out: "All unsaved in this house are going to hell. Life is just like a decayed limb of a tree to which you are clinging, and if it breaks, you who are unsaved will be in hell." . . . I therefore urged all to receive Jesus Christ as their Saviour, or else they would assuredly perish.

Never was there a more imperfect attempt at preaching; but never was there anything more sincere. Tears were many—words were few; but the results were marvellous. The Holy Spirit of God filled the place; the people were convicted of sin and their lost condition. . . . That night the work of God's grace had begun in many hearts.*

How we lack the passion of Christ on the cross. But with M'Kendrick, as soon as he was saved, fire began to burn within him. The spirit of the gospel is a sensing the perishing condition of sinners.

Six weeks later, the old missionary asked M'Kendrick to lead the meeting in one of three places.

I selected three of my companions to assist me. We had several rehearsals of our service, and much prayer. We each took our different parts—reading, singing, praying, and speaking. Three of us arranged to say a few words, but the major part was to be mine. Isaiah 53.5 was chosen as my text. I stuck very

Ibid., 32, 33.

close to my text, because I couldn't leave it. They got the pure Word of God that night, because I had nothing else to give them. Unlike my first attempt, I didn't scream, but the tears stole down my face all the time. As I kept repeating and reiterating— "He was wounded for our transgressions and bruised for our iniquities," God's Holy Spirit was using His Word both for convicting and converting. Some were saved and many were anxious, and we returned to our village too happy for words to describe, as we saw the fire kindled in Allanton that was then blazing in Ferniegair. *

Two years went by:

About this time I heard for the first time an evangelist preach. He held meetings every night for a month in Hamilton. His zeal for the lost and his success as a soul-winner were used by the Holy Spirit to create a greater passion for souls within me; and nightly as I walked from Hamilton to Ferniegair— nearly two miles distant—I kept [to] the centre of the road, my cap in hand, and prayed all the way to God that He would use me as a soul-winner. I had no desire to leave my ordinary work, for I was never happier in my life than when I wrought in the mines by day and preached the Gospel at night. . . .

It was a daily occurrence to hear of people being saved. I was then living in Hamilton, but working in Ferniegair. I had to leave for work about 4:45 a.m., and the streets being quiet at that hour, I carried a large piece of chalk and wrote in large letters striking texts upon the street pavement, such as— "Prepare to meet thy God," "Ye must be born again," "The wicked shall be turned into hell," etc., etc. God used those texts to awaken many. **

Ibid., 35–6.
**Ibid.*, 38, 40–1.

M'Kendrick continued:

The annual soiree was to be held in the Free Church, and only those who have lived in a small fishing village can fully understand all that such an event means for the church and people. The object is generally to raise funds for the church, and tickets for the occasion are sold at 1s. each. . . . As to the character of such gatherings, as a rule they are anything but serious. . . .

Mr. Paterson, the minister, was anxious that I should give an address at the soiree. I begged to be excused, on the plea that such occasions were not in my line. But he would take no refusal, [and] at last I consented. I earnestly prayed to God that I might have a suitable message, but the only subject that came to me was—"Ye must be born again." This I dismissed, knowing that such a text would not be in harmony with the occasion. But again and again this message returned. . . . When the evening arrived, I happily found that I was the fourth speaker on the programme, and that after my address there was an interval of fifteen minutes. . . . Amidst cheers and a terrific clapping of hands No. 3 came down, and I walked up. I was in God's hands, and how I prayed for His guidance. Results were God's part— obedience mine.

When the cheering had subsided, I said, "The first speaker who addressed you showed what all should do from the pulpit to the pew. I propose to take the same line, with this difference—I shall show what all '*must be*.' 'Ye *must* be born again.' " . . .

Beginning with the six ministers that were there, I showed how they could go to college without being born again, but not to heaven. They could graduate and take degrees without being born again; receive a call from a congregation, be ordained, and "wag their pow" in the pulpit without being born again. All this and much more they might do without being born again, but, reiterating my text, I repeated — "Except a man be born again he cannot enter into the kingdom of God." . . .

I then turned to the elders and deacons, and taking them in turn I detailed their duties — what they did and could do without being born again. I pointed out what solemn mockery it was for men to occupy a prominent place in a church who were not born again. By this time the silence of death filled the place, and the concern pictured on many faces plainly told that God's Holy Spirit was at work.

I then gave a few minutes to the church members — showing that they might eat of the bread — the symbol of His body given — and drink of the cup — the symbol of His blood once shed — without being born again. But, back again to my text, without the new birth there could be no admission to heaven.

I still had five minutes left for the choir, which sat immediately below me. They evidently knew their turn was coming, for immediately I said, "You can sing in the choir without being born again," they looked up and our eyes met. If ever I preached to a people with love in my heart and tears in my eyes, it was that night, and they could see and feel that it was no fanatical tirade or excited denunciation of their condition, but that it was a loving, faithful message out of a burdened heart.

Some said to me afterwards that they thought my remarks out of season. My reply was that I held a warrant for only two occasions — the one was to "preach in season," and the other "out of season."*

With the heart full of love and the eyes full of

Ibid., 106–11.

tears—this is the spirit of the gospel. We must feel deeply the love of God as well as the perishing of sinners.

In a certain fishing village, reported M'Kendrick, the hall was filled each night; earnest attention marked each service as the week went on, but as yet there was no manifest blessing. We had half an hour's prayer before the service, and the same after. By Thursday the impression had greatly deepened, and I felt sure the blessing was at hand. An aged woman prayed after the service that night. I wish the whole world could have heard that prayer— quiet, calm, and most restrained. She named many names to God—chiefly her relatives—with a few remarks about the condition and need of each one. Her own six sons she went over, one by one, and all the while the big tears rolled down her face. The other prayers that night were in harmony with this old woman's pleadings—all so natural and real.

That night I could not sleep: my soul was burdened with the lost. I saw men and women passing to perdition, only the beating of their heart keeping their body out of the grave and their soul out of hell. My restlessness awoke my wife. She said, "Are you not sleeping yet, Jim?" I said, "No, Maggie, I can't sleep, and I am sure there are others in Findochty who cannot sleep either. Let us rise and pray." And there we poured out our hearts to God, that He would graciously visit Findochty, as he had done Rosehearty.

Our prayer meeting prior to the service that night was a hallowed season such as I had never before experienced. The hall was full, and as I walked to the platform I was never so conscious of the presence of God. As I preached, the power of God fell upon the people, and up jumped a big man and cried aloud, "O God, save me, or I'll be in hell." For three or four minutes he continued to cry to God to save him. Turning to J.S. and A.S., I said, "If any of you know that man, you might go down and speak to him." He was now quiet, and leaning against the wall in an exhausted condition. I did not know A.S. was his father. The old man walked down the aisle, but as the seats were long and closely packed and the son was next the wall, he could not get near to him.

I wish I could reproduce the scene to my readers as it is photographed in my mind. Standing at the end of the seat he said, "Sanny, my son, put your trust in Jesus: He died for you. Trust yer faither's God. Oh, Sanny, my laddie, jist trust yer mither's Saviour."

While he was thus talking to his son, up jumped another man crying, "Lord, save me. I'm a cooart; I'm a cooart (coward). I should ha'e been saved at Wick, the time o' the great line fishing; but I wis a cooart — O Lord, I was a cooart; but I'll trust Ye noo."

As he sat down, another rose and stood on the seat, and he cried, "Oh, God, be merciful to me, the sinner. In the past I've been the Pharisee; but O Lord, this nicht Ye hiv let me see I'm a sinner. In the past I've seen everybody's fauts but my ain; but O Lord, Ye hiv let me see this nicht that every tub maun staun [tub must stand] on its ain bottom."

Christian friends pressed to shake hands and rejoice with these converts — all those related being especially jubilant; and the hearts of all God's people overflowed with praise. . . . But as we were leaving, the door was suddenly thrown open, and a tall young man came in and dropped full length on the floor before us. His anguish was pitiful; he had gone from the meeting in deep conviction, hoping that by so doing he would get quietness for his troubled mind; but around his fireside the scene in the hall was the subject of conversation, and this made him worse. He went to bed, thinking that there he would get relief; but the arrow had gone too deep to be eradicated that way. The awful thought constantly recurred to him — "If I die tonight, I'll be in hell." From his bedroom window he could see that the lights in the hall were being extinguished, and hurriedly pulling on his trousers only, he rushed back to the building, without boots or other clothing, and entered it as I have already described. Needless to add, God saved him . . . *

He who preaches the gospel must be filled with the love of Christ. His eyes will be full of tears. He will shout, for he sees the sufferings of sinners. He will pray to God because of the penalty he knows sinners will one day receive.

The gospel must live and develop in the spirit. If our spirit is usable, a right atmosphere will be created when the gospel is preached.

The love of God is something the world has never known. That Christ died to save is also beyond the reasoning of the world. The gospel is totally new to the world. There is no common ground between the gospel and the world.

Today the spirit of the gospel must burn like fire; otherwise, the gospel will be quenched by sinners. As the mouth is responsible for proclaiming the gospel, so the person is responsible for sending out the spirit of the gospel. The gospel must be like manna which is fresh every day. But for the spirit to launch forth,

---

Ibid., 122–5.

the outward man needs to be broken.

To send forth the truth of the gospel with the highest thought is but half the work. The other half is to touch sinners with the spirit of the gospel. He who loves himself has used up all his feelings on himself. We should learn to reserve our feeling for the gospel.

Fire need not be big, so long as it burns. The first one to be kindled is yourself. For the sake of the gospel, you need to be beside yourself before God like David of old was. You lay aside shame, glory and pride. All who are zealous in soul-winning are beside themselves for the gospel's sake.

The way people get saved is often according to the one who is used to save them. I would quote again from M'Kendrick's account:

> The Friday night of the second week in Port-knockie stands out as the most memorable in all my evangelistic career. The spirit of conviction was deep throughout the village, and there was an atmosphere of reverent solemnity everywhere that could be felt. That night after the address, I invited all who were anxious to remain—not one left. . . .
>
> Suddenly in the centre of the hall a man dropped on his knees, and cried, "O God, save me, be merciful to me a sinner." This poor man had a skin disease, and his appearance was to many (myself included) almost repulsive; but the minister assured me that behind that unsightly visage there was one of the brightest intellects in the village. As he moaned, and wept, and prayed for mercy, every eye in that place was dim, and many cheeks were wet with tears. After a few minutes, I drew near to him, and repeated what I thought appropriate texts, and then stepped back beside the minister.

That hour and scene live before me as I write; and I fervently wish that every infidel and unbeliever could have witnessed it. Slowly he raised his head, and that hitherto repulsive face was now radiant with the peace and grace of God. Still continuing upon his knees, he cried — "I'm saved; I'm saved. Oh, happy day! Oh, happy day! The Lord has washed my sins away." Then, rising to his feet, he said — "I'm saved, friends, I'm saved."

I can repeat his words, that is all my pen can do; but those who witnessed the scene will never forget it. Addressing the people, he said — "Last night I went to the pierhead, fully determined to jump in. I knew that because of my disease my outward appearance was offensive to you all — even to those who love me; and because of my sins, I felt I was offensive to God. Satan seemed to whisper within me, 'Neither God nor man wants you; put an end to it.' These have been the thoughts of my heart for the last two days, and as I stood on the pierhead last night, in great anguish of spirit — afraid to jump in, and too miserable to stay out — I can now see it was the voice of God saying, 'Don't jump in; go to the service tomorrow night again.' And here I am — saved. O praise God, I'm saved."

Tears were in his voice as well as in his eyes, as he thus spoke, and the whole company were greatly moved. He paused for a little, and no one seemed disposed to break the silence. He then prayed that "now that he was saved would God just take him home, and relieve him of his suffering? He was ready to go, and had no wish to stay." God answered his prayer, for in the course of three months, during which He allowed poor George to witness in a wondrous way to the saving power of His grace, his wish was fulfilled. . . .

When he finished his prayer in the hall, I said,

"You have heard this man's testimony, I have said all I can say, and it is now nearly eleven o'clock, and we must go." Many rose to leave, when a man jumped up and cried out, "Oh, praise God, I'm saved! There is no doubt about it — I feel it — I know it. I have been seeking salvation for years, but I have got it to-night." Then raising his hands above his head, and looking up, he cried, "O God, save everybody here. Oh, Lord, save everybody here." He then stepped on to a seat, and with his face shining, appealed to the people to trust in Christ, and be saved; and again he cried, "Lord, save the people."

. . . In less than five minutes over fifty people were on their knees upon the floor, crying to God for mercy. Over forty of these were men above thirty years of age. As one after another was born again and filled with the Holy Spirit, they literally danced for joy, and there was such a scene of excitement and religious fervour as no words can fitly set forth. I besought every saved person in the place to get outside, form into a procession, and give expression to their new-found joy by singing some hymns and marching through the village. . . . This continued on til 2:30 a.m., but even then many were too excited to go to rest. I have very imperfectly described that night, for it was the night of nights in my career, and in reviewing the extraordinary scenes of which I was an eyewitness on that occasion, I understood as never before how natural it was for ignorant onlookers on the day of Pentecost to imagine that those men on whom the Spirit descended were filled with wine. *

George Whitfield once said, "I preach as a dying

Ibid., 187-91.

man to a dying world." Sinners will be saved if we preach in such a spirit. The problem lies not in the scope of grace, which is unlimited, nor in the efficacy of the cross, for it is finished, but in us who block the flow of the gospel!

Part II

How to Preach the Gospel

One—About the Savior

The Lord Jesus is indeed the Savior of sinners, but He is also their Friend.

(1)*The Lord Jesus, the Savior of Sinners.* The Lord Jesus took up a body while on earth so that He could die on the cross for sinners, bearing their sins in His body; thus giving all who believe in Him forgiveness of sin. This was His prime motive on earth. His name, therefore, was called Jesus (Jehovah Savior). He today stands in the position of Savior to save us, the lost. He has provided full salvation for us. And as a result there is but one simple requirement made of us, which is to believe and be saved: repent and receive forgiveness: come and get rest: confess and be forgiven: "The word is nigh thee, in thy mouth, and in thy heart: . . . for with the heart man believeth unto righteousness; and with the mouth confession is made unto salvation" (Rom. 10. 8a, 10)—"He that will, let him take the water of life freely" (Rev. 22. 17d). In spite of its simple requirement, there are sinners who nonetheless feel they cannot believe. They will not repent, but rather love their sins. They will not come to the Savior. Even though it is right to present Jesus as Savior in the preaching of the gospel, a number of sinners who have problems are still being shut out. For the presentation of the Lord Jesus as the Savior of sinners is aimed at the need of those who will gladly accept Him.

(2) *The Lord Jesus, the Friend of Sinners.* The term "friend" conveys the idea of affection and love. It is the most unusual relationship among humankind. The relation between father and son is most intimate, but such a relationship is regular. Husband and wife love each other, but their position to each other is likewise normal. The relationship between servant and master, or between employee and employer is also something conventional. Only the relationship between friends is something informal and conducted on the basis of the same or equal position. A good father is not only that to his son but he is also his son's friend. A judge usually stands opposite to a criminal, yet some judges may even become criminals' friends. As friends, people may be able to pour out their hearts and openly reveal the real situation. They stand on the same footing towards each other. Now the relationship between God and men or between the Savior and sinners is formal. Although the Savior is good, what can a sinner such as I do if I cannot fulfill the requirement? This is why the Lord comes to be the sinner's Friend as well. He comes to help the sinners. He stands with them in order to help them come to the Savior. He causes those who are not able to believe to believe indeed in the Savior.

God was Abraham's Friend. Friendship transcends

position. When the father of the child with a dumb spirit cried out, "I believe; help thou mine unbelief" (Mark 9. 24b), this time the Lord served as the sinner's Friend. He gave the father faith to believe. Wherein did the young ruler do wrong in not being able to enter the kingdom of God? He did not ask the Lord for help. For "with men this is impossible; but with God all things are possible" (Matt. 19. 26b). The Lord Jesus is the sinner's Friend, therefore no one should fail to accept Him.

In the nineteenth century there was in London, England, a socialite. Her parents were titled persons, and hence she came from a family of nobility. She lived in a big mansion, and was young and beautiful. She was sought after by many gentlemen. Once at a big dancing party, she wore a specially tailored dress. That night she was the hit of the party. Towards dawn she returned home. She felt most unhappy. She threw her dress onto the chair and said, "If a Christian should meet me today, he would no doubt try to persuade me to believe in the Lord; but I will not believe." Yet later on, she knelt and prayed, "O God, if there is a God, I do not want You, nor will I believe in You. I do not believe You can give me joy. I do not have joy, but can You give me what I do not want?" As she got up, she was saved. Thus she found a Friend in Jesus who knew and supplied her need. She consecrated her life to the Lord at that very moment. Later, she was greatly used by the Lord.

In order to preach the Lord Jesus as the sinner's Friend, we must have power and revelation. The Lord Jesus *is* the sinner's Friend, yet, though some can *feel* it, others may not feel it that way.

It is the Lord as the sinner's Friend that moves people to repent and to believe. No sinner is without hope, for the Holy Spirit works upon every human heart. The Lord Jesus is truly the sinner's Friend as well as the sinner's Savior.

Two—The Condition of Salvation

Strictly speaking, salvation is without condition, for it is based on the grace of God in saving sinners. And since this is grace, there is neither work nor condition. But when we read the Bible, it would appear as though there were certain things the sinner must do. Let us presumably call them conditions—such things as repentence, confession and belief. One who preaches the gospel will naturally look for such conditions to be fulfilled, without which no one can be saved. So, he will encourage people to fulfill these presumed conditions.

It is very dangerous, however, to overly-emphasize these so-called conditions. For though the Bible does lay down these requirements quite clearly in certain passages, in some other passages they are not so clear but rather confusing. Ordinarily, repentance is the condition and forgiveness is the result; faith is the condition and eternal life the result. Yet in many places in the New Testament we find the condition and result are confused. Such confusion really serves God's purpose.

(1) "Repent ye, and be baptized every one of you in the name of Jesus Christ unto the remission of your sins" (Acts 2. 38a). Here, repentance is the condition for salvation. Yet in Acts 5. 31—"Him [Jesus Christ]

did God exalt with his right hand to be a Prince and a Saviour, to give repentance to Israel, and remission of sins"—both the condition of repentance and the resultant remission of sins are given by God. The Lord Jesus has accomplished the work of redemption on the cross so that God can apply salvation to the sinners.

(2) "Even the righteousness of God through faith in Jesus Christ unto all them that believe; for there is no distinction" (Rom. 3. 22). Faith is a condition. In the New Testament, faith is mentioned 150 times. In 2 Peter 1. 1b ("To them that have obtained a like precious faith with us in the righteousness of our God and the Saviour Jesus Christ"), however, faith is something obtained and it becomes the salvation. It is not what man gives to God; rather, it is what God gives to man. It is considered as part of the grace of God. How God is willing to do more for us!

(3) "A certain ruler asked him, saying, Good Teacher, what shall I do to inherit eternal life? And Jesus said unto him, Why callest thou me good? none is good, save one, even God. Thou knowest the commandments, Do not commit adultery, Do not kill, Do not steal, Do not bear false witness, Honor thy father and mother. And he said, All these things have I observed from my youth up. And when Jesus heard it, he said unto him, One thing thou lackest yet: sell all that thou hast, and distribute unto the poor, and thou shalt have treasure in heaven: and come, follow me. But when he heard these things, he became exceeding sorrowful; for he was very rich. And Jesus seeing him said, How hardly shall they that have riches enter into the kingdom of God! For it is easier for a camel to enter in through a needle's

eye, than for a rich man to enter into the kingdom of God. And they that heard it said, Then who can be saved? But he said, The things which are impossible with men are possible with God" (Luke 18. 18–27). "Zaccheus stood, and said unto the Lord, Behold, Lord, the half of my goods I give to the poor; and if I have wrongfully exacted aught of any man, I restore fourfold. And Jesus said unto him, Today is salvation come to this house, forasmuch as he also is a son of Abraham" (Luke 19. 8–9). To sell all is a condition set forth in Luke 18 for gaining eternal life. In Luke 19, however, selling or giving away all is itself salvation.

(4) "Behold, a certain lawyer stood up and made trial of him, saying, Teacher, what shall I do to inherit eternal life? And he said unto him, What is written in the law? how readest thou? And he answering said, Thou shalt love the Lord thy God with all thy heart, and with all thy soul, and with all thy strength, and with all thy mind; and thy neighbor as thyself. And he said unto him, Thou hast answered right: this do, and thou shalt live" (Luke 10. 25–28). Here our Lord answered the lawyer's first question by saying that to love one's neighbor is a *condition* for having eternal life. But in answering his second question, "And who is my neighbor?" (v. 29b), our Lord made loving the neighbor the *consequence*, instead of the condition, of salvation. The lawyer thought of himself as the good Samaritan, but the Lord said that the lawyer was the one who went down from Jerusalem to Jericho and fell into the hands of the robbers (Jerusalem means "peace" whereas Jericho means "curse"). When the Lord said to the lawyer, "Go, and do thou likewise" (v. 37b), He

was telling him to love the Savior who was the good Samaritan.

(5) "One of the Pharisees desired him that he would eat with him. And he entered into the Pharisee's house, and sat down to meat. And behold, a woman who was in the city, a sinner; and when she knew that he was sitting at meat in the Pharisee's house, she brought an alabaster cruse of ointment, and standing behind at his feet, weeping, she began to wet his feet with her tears, and wiped them with the hair of her head, and kissed his feet, and anointed them with the ointment. Now when the Pharisee that had bidden him saw it, he spake within himself, saying, This man, if he were a prophet, would have perceived who and what manner of woman this is that toucheth him, that she is a sinner. . . . When they had not wherewith to pay, he forgave them both. Which of them therefore will love him most? [v. 42] . . . And turning to the woman, he said unto Simon, Seest thou this woman? . . . Wherefore I say unto thee, Her sins, which are many, are forgiven; for she loved much: but to whom little is forgiven, the same loveth little [v. 47]. And he said unto her, Thy sins are forgiven [v. 48]. . . . And he said unto the woman, Thy faith hath saved thee; go in peace" (Luke 7. 36–39, 42, 44, 47–48, 50). Here the consequence of salvation becomes the condition of salvation. It is quite different from the foregoing two conditions. In verse 42, it is being forgiven first and then loving the lender. But in verses 47 and 48, we find that her being forgiven is due to her loving much. Forgiveness follows love, and yet he who is forgiven little loves little. Hence the content of salvation is also the condition of salvation. As a matter of

fact, the condition of salvation is living and flexible rather than rigid and fixed.

(6) "Come unto me, all ye that labor and are heavy laden, and I will give you rest" (Matt. 11. 28); for "the Son of man came to seek and to save that which was lost" (Luke 19. 10). If you cannot come to Him, He will come to you: The Lord came into the house of Zacchaeus.

(7) "Ye will not come to me, that ye may have life" (John 5. 40). People will not come to the Lord to receive life. But "he that will, let him take the water of life freely" (Rev. 22. 17d). "As many as received him, to them gave he the right to become children of God, even to them that believe on his name: who were born, not of blood, nor of the will of the flesh, nor of the will of man, but of God" (John 1.12-13). Come just as you are.

(8) "I am the good shepherd: the good shepherd layeth down his life for the sheep. . . . But ye believe not, because ye are not of my sheep" (John 10. 11, 26). The Good Shepherd lays down His life for His sheep. First, be His sheep, then believe in Him. To be a sheep is salvation, to believe is the condition. First salvation, and then the condition.

(9) "And that in the good ground, these are such as in an honest and good heart, having heard the word, hold it fast, and bring forth fruit with patience" (Luke 8. 15). The good ground is the honest and good heart. Yet we are told that "the heart is deceitful above all things, and it is exceedingly corrupt: who can know it? (Jer. 17. 9) It is the Holy Spirit who creates in such a heart honesty and goodness, making it good ground. This is therefore the contents of salvation as well as the

condition of salvation. In the Epistles, we find that goodness is the fruit of the Holy Spirit.

Never try to look for the conditions of salvation in a sinner. For the weakness of a sinner is the very strength whereby to receive salvation. The Lord became primarily the Friend of the sinner, and He never is bound by any condition.

Three—The Two Sides of the Gospel

On the one side, how does a sinner receive the gospel; on the other side, how does God provide the gospel? One pertains to the experience of the sinner, while the other presents the truth of the gospel. In the four Gospels and Acts we see how the gospel is preached and received by sinners, but in the Epistles we are given understanding as to what the gospel is. On the one hand we are shown how people experience the gospel—that is to say, how salvation comes upon men. On the other hand we are shown how God satisfies His own demand. When God comes to save, His forgiveness is lawful and righteous. For the redemption of the Lord Jesus has already satisfied all the demands of God. The Lord Jesus "was delivered up for our trespasses, and was raised for our justification" (Rom. 4. 25). The Holy Spirit then comes to apply the finished work of Christ to us, so as to become our subjective experience. The work of the Holy Spirit is to translate the objective to be subjective, to turn doctrine into experience.

There are two different approaches in the preaching of the gospel: (1) tell the sinners how the work of the Lord Jesus has satisfied God's demand. The purpose of such preaching of the gospel is to make known to sinners the nature of the gospel. And (2) lead the sinners to the place where the Holy Spirit is able to apply the work of Christ upon them. Such preaching of the gospel is for acceptance, not for understanding.

Read the Epistles in order to understand what the gospel is, for they commence with God and reveal the contents of the gospel. Study the four Gospels and Acts to learn the way of preaching the gospel, because they begin with sinners and show the consequence of the gospel.

How does the Holy Spirit work? And how did our Lord and the apostles save souls?

(1) "He said unto her, Thy sins are forgiven. . . . And he said unto the woman, Thy faith hath saved thee; go in peace" (Luke 7. 48, 50). How were her sins forgiven? Her faith saved her. She did not understand much about doctrines, but her heart was attracted to the Lord. She loved Him. She just wept, and she felt the loveliness of the Lord. And hence, her salvation was due to her heart being drawn to the Lord.

(2) "He said unto her, Daughter, thy faith hath made thee whole; go in peace" (Luke 8. 48). The woman with an issue of blood was not only healed but also saved. The Lord said to her, "Thy faith hath made thee whole; go in peace." This word refers also to inward salvation. The same is true with the word which our Lord spoke to one of the ten lepers who were cured, "Thy faith hath made thee whole" (Luke 17. 19b), which word implies *spiritual* healing in addition to physical healing. The gratitude of the one cured touched the heart of the Lord.

(3) "For this my son was dead, and is alive again; he was lost, and is found" (Luke 15. 24a). The prodigal son was saved because of a change in his mind. His heart turned back to his father. Though he entertained the thought of being a hired servant, the father (representing God) granted him forgiveness liberally and abundantly.

(4) "I say unto you, This man went down to his house justified rather than the other: for every one that exalteth himself shall be humbled; but he that humbleth himself shall be exalted" (Luke 18. 14). This publican was justified (in the Gospels, he is the only one recorded as being justified). He stood afar off and dared not so much as to lift up his eyes to heaven. He had no knowledge of the contents of the gospel. He only had a desire. He asked with timidity, and yet he was justified.

(5) "He made haste, and came down, and received him [Jesus] joyfully. . . . And Jesus said unto him, To-day is salvation come to this house, forasmuch as he also is a son of Abraham" (Luke 19. 6, 9). Zacchaeus wished to see the Lord. Was it mere curiosity or was it an unexplainable longing? He was ignorant of three things—he had no feeling of guilt, he had no knowledge of the contents of the gospel, and he did not know who the Lord was. He just had a desire to see the Lord. But as soon as he made contact with the Lord, he said, "Behold, Lord, the half of my goods I give to the poor; and if I have wrongfully exacted aught of any man, I restore fourfold" (v. 8b). He confessed the Lord as well as confessed his sins by promising to make restitution. He came into the good of salvation for Jesus declared that he was also a son of Abraham. All the works of

salvation are indeed for the satisfaction of all the demands of God.

(6) "He said, Jesus, remember me when thou comest in thy kingdom. And he said unto him, Verily I say unto thee, To-day shalt thou be with me in Paradise" (Luke 23. 42–43). At the beginning of the crucifixion, both robbers mocked the Lord. But one of them listened to the Lord's prayer on the cross, "Father, forgive them, for they know not what they do" (v. 34a). He began to change. First, he believed in God; next, he had a sense of sinfulness; and finally, he had a little understanding of the Lord. He recognized that the Lord was righteous. He did not even know how to cry out, "Lord"; but his heart had touched the Lord. Though the wording of his prayer was inaccurate, he was nonetheless to be in Paradise with all those saved souls.

(7) "Jesus answered and said unto her, If thou knewest the gift of God, and who it is that saith to thee, Give me to drink; thou wouldest have asked of him, and he would have given thee living water" (John 4. 10). In order to lead this woman to faith, our Lord asked her instead for water to drink. He only made the woman see her need, without even telling her how He would die for her. As soon as a person comes into contact with Christ, that person is saved.

(8) "She said, No man, Lord. And Jesus said, Neither do I condemn thee: go thy way; from henceforth sin no more" (John 8. 11). She got saved in a special way. All those who would condemn her had slipped away. The woman had committed sin and was waiting for judgment. Our Lord was without sin, therefore He did not, like the others, slink away. In hearing the Lord

say, "Woman, where are they? did no man condemn thee?" (v. 10b), she was brought to her sense of guilt. And hence she said, ". . . Lord." How beautiful is this word, "Lord."

(9) "He answered and said, And who is he, Lord, that I may believe on him? Jesus said unto him, Thou hast both seen him, and he it is that speaketh with thee. And he said, Lord, I believe. And he worshipped him" (John 9. 36–38). The blind man had his eyes opened. All he knew about the Lord was revealed in verses 31 and 33: "We know that God heareth not sinners: but if any man be a worshipper of God, and do his will, him he heareth. . . . If this man were not from God, he could do nothing." He had revelation in his spirit, so he addressed Jesus as "Lord." But his mind was unfruitful. Therefore he asked who the Son of God was. And with just a little enlightening from the Lord, he got saved.

(10) "Let all the house of Israel therefore know assuredly, that God hath made him both Lord and Christ, this Jesus whom ye crucified" (Acts 2. 36). How were the three thousand souls saved on the day of Pentecost? In Peter's message, the first section explains the experience of Pentecost, and the second section narrates how the Lord, after having been crucified by the people, was raised from among the dead. The climax in the release of Peter's spirit comes in his declaration to the house of Israel that God has made Jesus, whom they crucified, both Lord and Christ. When they heard this, they were pricked in their heart.

(11) "Peter opened his mouth, and said, Of a truth I perceive that God is no respecter of persons . . . To

him bear all the prophets witness, that through his name every one that believeth on him shall receive remission of sins" (Acts 10. 34, 43). Peter merely related the fact of salvation; he had not yet spoken on the doctrine of salvation. But the Holy Spirit fell on all those who heard the word.

To sum up, salvation is based on the finished work of Christ on the cross. Its coming to men does not depend on men's understanding. On the one hand, it is essential for God to know and thus to accept the work of Christ. For men, on the other hand, so long as they contact Christ, they are saved. The Epistles reveal to us the contents of the gospel, but the four Gospels and Acts show us how people touch the Lord and get saved. Therefore, in preaching the gospel, we must learn the way, as demonstrated in the Gospels and Acts, as to how to lead people to be in touch with the Lord.

Four — How Sinners Receive the Gospel

People are saved through many and varied experiences. By analyzing these experiences, we find that four factors must not be missing; otherwise, people will not be saved. These four factors are: (1) Need — such as a sense of sin, or a sense of discontent. (2) Desire — a desire from the heart. (3) Knowledge of God — a knowledge of at least something about the Lord's work or His salvation. (4) Action — such as to believe, to confess sins, repent, or receive. All who are truly saved will have experienced these four factors — nothing less, but perhaps even more. So that whoever is preaching the gospel must pay attention to these four factors.

Creating a sense of need in people (1), as well as stirring up a desire from their heart (2), and, also, causing them to know something about the Lord (3) — these three factors belong to the time of casting the gospel net. Helping people to take action (4) pertains to drawing the net. Let us look at each of these four factors more closely.

Five — The Sense of Need

The sense of need includes (1) a sense of discontent, and (2) a sense of sin. It is appropriate to take the road to a sense of sin in relation to nominal Christians; but in relation to ordinary nonbelievers, it is more effective to take the road to vanity.

There is a basic difference between the Jews and the Chinese: the first group have a natural sense of sinning against God, but the second do not possess such a sense. Idol-worship to the Chinese is purely a matter of looking for blessing. It is fundamentally a "bless me" premise. Even the thieves and the prostitutes in our Chinese society have their idols to worship, but they do not have a sense of sin. Among the Chinese, only an elite class of rationalists have experienced some sort of inability in overcoming sin, similar to the experience described in Romans 7; and yet even *they* do not have the overwhelming sense of sins that is discussed in Romans 1–3.

A. Concerning *the sense of discontent*, five points should be emphasized:

(1) *A sense of toil, pain and unrest.* "Come unto me, all ye that labor and are heavy laden, and I will give you rest" (Matt. 11. 28). This approach is most effec-

tive towards the middle-aged and the old-aged people. According to church statistics kept over several hundred years of experience, the number of people who have been saved under the preaching of Matthew 11. 28 is equal to that of people saved under the preaching of John 3. 16.

(2) *The vanities of the world.* As in John 4, all who drink the water of this world will never be satisfied. The joy which our Lord gives alone satisfies, for it shall become in men a well of water springing up to eternal life. Those who drink of this water shall never be thirsty again. Christians are not a people who try to attain happiness through contentment; rather, the joy of the Lord within them causes them to be fully satisfied.

(3) *What the meaning of life is.* Men are not only created *by* God, they are also created *for* God, because God is actually the center of mankind. Those who are unsaved find life to be tasteless. Only those who have found God find joy and rest. Just as all the created things on earth are held together by the power of gravity in the physical sense, even so are all created things being kept by the power of God in the moral sense. If the gravitational force were to disappear, all things would lose their meaning and coordination, and all things would be thrown into chaos. Similarly, without having God as the center, mankind would be reduced to utter confusion too.

(4) *Death.* How transient and temporary human life is! One third of man's life is spent in sleep; one sixth, in eating; and one third in working. What time there is left for enjoyment is but little. Yet paradoxically, it is equally hard to die. For a Christian, he has no fear

of death. He dies peacefully and joyfully for he longs to meet his Lord, which is very far better. A nonbeliever, however, is afraid of death for he is terrified by the darkness ahead of him. The Lord Jesus came that He "might deliver all them who through fear of death were all their lifetime subject to bondage" (Heb. 2. 15).

(5) *The Coming Judgment.* The Chinese have some idea of the coming judgment. They have the concept of hell. It is therefore possible to use this approach in preaching the gospel. What about the coming judgment? What about hades after death, and even hell, the second death? Some people cannot be touched by love, but they will be moved by fear. Some take action out of faith; some out of love; while some, out of fear.

B. Concerning *the sense of sin*, five points need also to be stressed:

(1) *The power of sin.* Romans 7 may be used to demonstrate how human resolution and suppresion of the old man cannot overcome the power of sin.

(2) *Seeing our sins through the mirror of the sins of other people.* A person may sin without feeling sinful, but he can easily sense sins committed by other people. Hence, it is possible to lead a person to realize his own sins by showing him the sins of others. Paul himself did this: "Reckonest thou this, O man, who judgest them that practise such things, and doest the same, that thou shalt escape the judgment of God?" (Rom. 2. 3)

(3) *The penalty of sin.* "He that soweth unto his own flesh shall of the flesh reap corruption" (Gal. 6. 8a). The one who sins shall eat the fruit of his sin. "The

way of the transgressor is hard" (Prov. 13. 15b). "He that sinneth against me [i.e., against Wisdom, a personification of God] wrongeth his own soul: all that hate me love death" (Prov. 8. 36).

(4) *Sinning against man is sinning against God.* David sinned against Uriah the Hittite by having him murdered, but he realized that he had in the same act sinned against God: "I know my transgressions; and my sin is ever before me. Against thee [God], thee only, have I sinned, and done that which is evil in thy sight" (Ps. 51. 3-4). David was unrighteous and unlovely towards man, but in so doing he was also being rebellious and unfaithful towards God. God is high above all, for all authorities belong to Him. All who sin against man sin at the same time against God. God had given David authority and power, but David abused that which God had given him.

The greatest sin is that done against God. For example, the story was told about a widow who brought up her son by washing people's clothing. She had much earlier rescued her son when their house had caught fire. As a consequence, she had been badly burned, and her face had become marred and repulsive in appearance. One day she encountered her son as he was walking on the street with some of his classmates. She beckoned to her son, but her son was too ashamed to own her as his mother, she being so shabbily dressed and ugly-looking. In passing, she heard her son telling his friends that this was his maid in the house. The mother's heart was broken. How much more sinful it is for men to disown God!

(5) *Unbelief is sin.* "He [the Holy Spirit], when he

is come, will convict the world in respect of sin . . . : of sin, because they believe not on me [Christ Jesus]" (John 16. 8a, 9). In the story of the prodigal son told of in Luke 15, the prodigal had left home and hurt his father's heart of love; nevertheless, his father still loved him and cared about him, and received him with abundant grace upon his return home. All this indicates that God loves to show grace in saving souls. He will not hold anything against us. Hence, unbelief is a serious sin against God. "God so loved the world, that he gave his only begotten Son, that whosoever believeth on him, should not perish, but have eternal life" (John 3. 16). To misunderstand, even reject, God's love is a greater sin than to kill.

Six—Some Knowledge of God

Concerning the knowledge of God, there are, minimally, four things sinners ought to know:

(1) *Know that God is a Father who especially loves to answer prayers.* Setting aside the matter of creation, insofar as redemption is concerned, we know there is a difference between Father in the truth and Father in the gospel. According to the truth, God is Father only to those who have believed in the Lord Jesus and have received eternal life. People of the world are not God's children, rather they are children of the devil. "As many as received him [Jesus Christ], to them gave he the right to become children of God, even to them that believe on his name: who were born, not of blood, nor of the will of the flesh, nor of the will of man, but of God" (John 1. 12–13). These verses show us most clearly that,

redemptively speaking, only those who are born of God are the children of God.

Nevertheless, in preaching the gospel, it is altogether proper to tell the sinner that God is his Father. This is the Father as in the gospel, not as in the matter of truth and fact. For God does indeed treat a sinner as a father treats his own child. Such a figurative saying also anticipates the future. The story of the prodigal son presupposes his returning home to his father. This is the first proposition.

"Ask, and it shall be given you; seek, and ye shall find; knock, and it shall be opened unto you; for every one that asketh receiveth; and he that seeketh findeth; and to him that knocketh it shall be opened. Or what man is there of you, who, if his son shall ask him for a loaf, will give him a stone; or if he shall ask for a fish, will give him a serpent? If ye then, being evil, know how to give good gifts unto your children, how much more shall your Father who is in heaven give good things to them that ask him? All things therefore whatsoever ye would that men should do unto you, even so do ye also unto them: for this is the law and the prophets" (Matt. 7. 7–12). God is therefore the God who hears prayers. "He that cometh to God must believe that he is, and that he is a rewarder of them that seek after him" (Heb. 11. 6b). This, then, is the second proposition.

In the parable of Luke 15, the father was found anxiously waiting for the prodigal son to come home. Our heavenly Father is much more concerned about our future than even our own self. In the history of the church evangel, Luke 15 has been greatly used in saving souls.

(2) *Know that God has a gift to give.* "Jesus answered and said unto her, If thou knowest the gift of God, and who it is that saith to thee, Give me to drink; thou wouldest have asked of him, and he would have given thee living water" (John 4. 10). If you had known the gift of God, you would have asked of Him. Unfortunately, many know of God but they do not know the gift of God. People need to know the gift of God. For God's gift is not only that which will satisfy all their needs, it is also that which is eternal and unchanging. The basic thought in John 4 is concerned with the gift which is given freely to men.

Now when the special need of God's gift in a sinner is found out, it is essential to give him a Scripture verse. For example, for a person who has no rest, share with him Matthew 11. 28: "Come unto me, all ye that labor and are heavy laden, and I will give you rest." Or if he has no peace, give him Philippians 4. 7: "the peace of God, which passeth all understanding, shall guard your hearts and your thoughts in Christ Jesus." Or if he is afraid of judgment, present him with John 5. 24: "Verily, verily, I say unto you, He that heareth my word, and believeth him that sent me, hath eternal life, and cometh not into judgment, but hath passed out of death into life." Show him that his name is now written in the book of life. Or if he is fearful of death, quote him 1 Corinthians 15. 57 ("Thanks be to God, who giveth us the victory through our Lord Jesus Christ") or Hebrews 2. 14 ("Since then the children are sharers in flesh and blood, he also himself in like manner partook of the same; that through death he might bring to nought him that had the power of death, that is, the devil").

(3) *Know the Lord Jesus.* It is absolutely necessary to know who Jesus is. Simply put, Jesus is the Son of God as well as the Christ of God (this knowledge includes the fact that Jesus is the Savior). The woman taken in adultery called Jesus, "Lord" (John 8. 11). Zacchaeus called Jesus, "Lord" (Luke 19. 8) When Saul (later named Paul) was enlightened on the road to Damascus, he also called Jesus, "Lord" (Acts 9. 5). "No man can say, Jesus is Lord, but in the Holy Spirit" (1 Cor. 12. 3b). The Holy Spirit alone enables people to call Jesus, "Lord."

(4) *Know Redemption.* The woman told of in Luke 7 who wept had the inward sense of being forgiven much. The prayer of the publican was: "God, be thou merciful to me a sinner" (Luke 18. 13b), which could legitimately be translated as: "God, allow me to have my sins atoned for." The robber on the cross knew that Christ suffered for the sake of others. For "apart from shedding of blood there is no remission" (Heb. 9. 22b); "Christ also suffered for sins once, the righteous for the unrighteous, that he might bring us to God" (1 Peter 3. 18a); "who his own self bare our sins in his body upon the tree, that we, having died unto sins, might live unto righteousness" (1 Peter 2. 24); and, "being justified freely by his grace through the redemption that is in Christ Jesus: whom God set forth to be a propitiation, through faith, in his blood, to show his righteousness" (Rom. 3. 24–25a).

It is also appropriate to mention something about resurrection: "who was delivered up for our trespasses, and was raised for our justification" (Rom. 4.25). Resurrection is the proof that our sins have been atoned for.

Hence it serves as the evidence of our justification. The resurrection of the Savior indicates that God's demands upon us for having sinned against Him have all been satisfied. Thus we are able to come before God, asking for forgiveness and gift.

To sum up, the minimum requirements in the knowledge of God in the gospel are (1) to know God, (2) to know God as the Giver of gift, (3) to know the Lord Jesus, and (4) to know the redemption of Christ.

Seven — How to Cause People to Desire

"And that in the good ground, these are such as in an honest and good heart, having heard the word, hold it fast, and bring forth fruit with patience" (Luke 8. 15). The seed is the word of the gospel, and the good ground is the heart of man. It is with the heart that we receive the word. Such a heart needs to have the two basic qualities of being honest and good. The apostle Paul said the same thing: "Believe in thy heart . . . : for with the heart man believeth unto righteousness" (Rom. 10. 9b, 10a). Unbelief is due to "an evil heart of unbelief" (Heb. 3. 12).

As in our physical body there is the heart (Gk. *kardia*), so in our spiritual and moral being there is also the heart. The heart is the seat of personality. It is the rendezvous of the spirit and soul and body: "out of it [the heart] are the issues of life" (Prov. 4. 23b). In the heart is the inner man; and conscience is the conscience of the heart.

What are the conditions of a sinner's heart? A person gets saved not initially through the body nor even through the spirit (for his spirit is dead due to sins and transgressions). It is his heart that must receive the word. Yet "the heart is deceitful above all things, and it is exceedingly corrupt: who can know it?" (Jer. 17. 9) A man's heart is bound up with sin, and its functions — such as understanding (or discernment), desire and decision — are very corrupt. (1) As to the *understanding* of the heart of an unsaved person, it is described in Romans 1: "because that knowing God, they glorified him not as God, neither gave thanks; but became vain in their reasonings, and their senseless heart was darkened" (v.21). (2) As to the *desire* of a sinner's heart, we are told that "there is none that understandeth, there is none that seeketh after God" (Rom. 3. 11). "None that understandeth" is due to the darkened mind. "None that seeketh" means there is no *desire* after God. Sinful man has no feeling towards God. Hence our Lord once said (quoting from the Psalms): "They hated me without a cause" (John 15. 25b). (3) And as to the *decision* of the unsaved one's heart, this we learn from the Scriptures: "Ye *will not* come to me, that ye may have life," said Jesus (John 5. 40). A man's will makes the final decision, but he will not come to God. Jesus cried out and lamented as follows: "O Jerusalem, Jerusalem, that killeth the prophets, and stoneth them that are sent unto her! how often would I have gathered thy children together, even as a hen gathereth her chickens under her wings, and ye *would not!*" (Matt. 23. 37)

The words in Matthew 13. 15 support the above observations: "this people's heart is waxed gross, and their ears are dull of hearing, and their eyes they have closed; lest haply they should perceive with their eyes, and hear with their ears, and understand with their heart, and should turn again, and I should heal them."

Of the three problems of a sinner's heart, the greatest one is in the region of desire (the second point above). Hence the greatest work in preaching the gospel is to reach and stir up the desire of a sinner. And the final work is to touch his will in making the decision. Let us look closely as to how this latter work is to be done.

(1) *Enlighten the mind.* The understanding, desire and decision of a sinner are all exceedingly corrupt. The whole world is under darkness. But as the word of God enters man's mind, it gains a foothold there. His heart undergoes a split. On the one hand, it rejects the word; on the other hand, it is nonetheless willing to accept the word. So that the hearing of the gospel is the starting point of salvation. To shed some light (the word of God) in man's mind is therefore the first step of the work. Words of enlightenment such as the sinner's judgment, the penalty of sin, and so forth, could be used as the Holy Spirit leads.

(2) *Create the desire of the heart.* When the mind is darkened, there is absolutely no desire for God in the heart. Use the word of God as well as the testimonies of the saved to stir up the sinner's heart desire for the gospel. God's love, the vanity of the world, the loss of the soul in spite of the gain of the world, and so on, can all be used by the Holy Spirit to create a heart desire in a sinner.

(3) *Help the will to decide.* After a person's desire

is stirred up, the next step is to encourage him to make a decision for the gospel. "He that is wise winneth souls" (Prov. 11. 30b). It takes wisdom to save souls.

From the mind to the emotion and then to the will—this is the mechanism for causing a sinner to desire and to decide for salvation. And in this subjective process, our Lord Jesus becomes the Friend of sinners. He influences people to desire after salvation.

"An honest and good heart" (Luke 8. 15). Some hearts may be honest but not good. It is true that God does not want people to pretend. He would rather have people acknowledge that they love sins. This is being honest. But He wants people to be good, that is to say, He wants them to desire after Him. He will hear those who pray, "O Lord, cause me not to love sins but to believe in You. Make me to desire after You." This is being good, this is having a good heart.

Eight—Lead to Action

We shall look at this final factor by means of four steps:

(1) *Lead to confess sins before God.* "If we confess our sins, he is faithful and righteous to forgive us our sins, and to cleanse us from all unrighteousness" (1 John 1. 9).

(a) Confession here does not have reference to people standing before an assembly and confessing their sins. Confession is directed towards God. It is to confess before Him. A sinner must be brought to the Lord. He is not saved until he meets his Savior. The gospel needs to be preached with clarity, yet even clarity in gospel preaching is no substitute for contact between the sinner and the Savior. To be in touch with the Lord is the first order of salvation, while to preach the gospel clearly is but the second order. A sinner is not only to be led to the gospel feast, he must also be brought face to face with the Host of the feast.

(b) Confession is to confess sins before God. All the works of a sinner are sinful in the sight of God. He is to confess "all unrighteousness, wickedness, covetousness, maliciousness; full of envy, murder, strife, deceit, malignity, whisperers, backbiters, hateful to God, insolent, haughty, boastful, inventors of evil things, disobedient to parents, without understanding, covenant-breakers, without natural affection, unmerciful" (Rom. 1. 29–31). As he confesses, he asks for God's forgiveness, since forgiveness is based on confession. Condemning sin as sin at the beginning results in being delivered from the sin he has confessed.

To confess sin is to condemn sin as sin. It is to stand on God's side against the adversary, Satan.

(c) The principle of confession is that the sinner presents himself with his sins before God. Do not have the false idea that a person sends his sins to God first and then he comes afterwards. No, the sinner himself comes with his sins. The first time a person meets God, he brings his sins with him; otherwise, he cannot see God.

(d) Confess two kinds of sins. Confess the kind one has forsaken and the kind that still remains unforsaken. F. B. Meyer once prayed: "O Lord, what I am unwilling, make me willing to be willing."

(2) *Give a special word of God.* Always have a

number of suitable Bible verses in store. Learn to use these words of God skillfully. After prayerful consideration, read an appropriate verse or verses to the sinner. For people are saved not just because of their confession of sins, but also because they receive the word of God: "They then that received his word were baptized: and there were added unto them in that day about three thousand souls" (Acts 2. 41). Without God's word, there is no basis for forgiveness: "Receive with meekness the implanted word, which is able to save your souls" (James 1. 21b). For there to be the salvation of the soul, there must be the implanted word: "he hath granted unto us his precious and exceeding great promises; that through these ye may become partakers of the divine nature, having escaped from the corruption that is in the world by lust" (2 Peter 1.4). It is through God's precious and exceeding great promises (found in His written word) that we may become partakers of the divine nature: "These things have I written unto you, that ye may know that ye have eternal life, even unto you that believe on the name of the Son of God" (1 John 5.13). How can we know we have eternal life if we do not have the word?

With God's word there is also His work. Whoever accepts the word of God accepts the work of God as well. Accordingly, in talking with a sinner, it is wise to read the word of God slowly. Read till light breaks forth. Having a word is like having a pillow upon which one may lay one's head and go to sleep. "If we confess our sins, he is faithful and righteous to forgive us our sins, and to cleanse us from all unrighteousness" (1 John 1. 9). Here is the word for both the forgiving and the cleansing.

(3) *Cause to believe in God's word.* When a person believes, he believes not only in the gospel, he believes also in the word of God. With God's word, he is able to approach God as well as deal with the devil. Faith is the believing in God's word, while confession is a personal act. I do my part, and God does His part. According to 1 John 1. 9, what a person must do is to confess his sins, and what God will do is to forgive and to cleanse. Faith is like the signing of a contract between two parties. I must fulfill my obligation in order for God to fulfill His. Since God is more righteous and faithful than I am, He will not fail to perform His promise. Faith thus sees the Unseen by trusting in God's word. Our Lord said to the woman who had an issue of blood: "Daughter, thy faith hath made thee whole; go in peace" (Mark 5. 34). This word not only healed her but also saved her. She could use this word to overcome temptation and trials throughout her life thereafter.

(4) *Test the faith.* The ways of testing include open confession of the Lord as well as baptism: (a) "with the mouth confession is made unto salvation" (Rom. 10. 10b). Many people before they openly confess the Lord are rather hazy about their salvation, but once they stand up and confess, they become clear. Likewise, (b) before their baptism they are not so sure, but after baptism they are firmly grounded. As water solidifies the cement, so baptism seals their faith.

Nine — Some Questions and Answers

(1) Should the preaching of "vanities" be directed to the aged?

True, this arrow is most effective with the older people, yet we should not be too conscious of age lest it produce self-love.

(2) Are "hell" and "the lake of fire" the same?

Hell is the same as the lake of fire, but with the Chinese, the concept of hell is more easily understood.

(3) How many approaches can we use in preaching the gospel?

There are six approaches we may employ: (a) sin, (b) hell or judgment, (c) the vanities of the world, (d) the love of God, (e) the righteousness of God (God saves us according to His righteousness; before the cross it is all love, but after the cross it is righteousness; God cannot but save us because He is righteous), and (f) the way of living faith (help people to come before God in prayer).

(4) How do we present the gospel?

The contents of the gospel presented must be rich. Use twenty minutes to speak clearly with words of understanding. At the appropriate time, let the spirit be released. When the spirit comes forth, sometimes you shout, but sometimes you cry. As we have mentioned before, James M'Kendrick was Scottish. The Scottish temperament is rather cold and aloof. But when he saw sinners he wept, because the spirit of the gospel was in him. George Whitfield said, "I am a dying man preaching to a dying world." And M'Kendrick himself declared:

> I have done a good deal of trout fishing in my day, and the fly that caught the most was the one I used the most. The same with my sermons—those I find that God blesses most, these I use frequently. We

all have to answer to our own Master, and each servant must be fully persuaded in his own mind as to his mode of procedure.*

Without the release of the spirit it is impossible to send a word into the sinner's heart. It is a fundamental error for us to think that we must beg people to receive Christ if it appears the Holy Spirit is neither working nor blessing. The fact of the matter is that the Holy Spirit *will* work and He is *willing* to bless if He can find *a useful vessel.* Evan Roberts once said, "Do not ask the Holy Spirit to work. For I have found a law that if I fulfill God's requirement, His blessing will come." And thus was Roberts used in the breaking out of the great Welsh revival of 1903–04.

For the church to preach the gospel, she must have the Sword of the Spirit. Prepare a number of Bible verses and get the brothers and sisters to memorize them. As we have previously mentioned, there are four steps in helping people towards accepting the gospel; namely, (1) sense or feeling, (2) knowledge, (3) desire, and (4) action. All those who assist in the preaching of the gospel must discern what step the sinners are at and help them accordingly. The greatest problem lies in the third step, that is to say, the creation of a heart desire for the gospel. Unless there is the spirit of the gospel in the preacher, it is impossible to incline a human heart towards such desire.

(5) Since the approach used in preaching the gospel varies, is it better to develop one's own approach instead of imitating that of others?

---

*Ibid., 182.

Beware of human manufacturing. He who has the fire within cannot help but let it burn. It is unnatural for one to weep when he is not weeping inwardly; nor is it natural for one to shout if he is not shouting within. To imitate the manner of others is equal to a lie in the area of action. If things are real, there will not be self-consciousness. If false, it is like theatrical acting which for this purpose is most ugly. In order to determine which to adopt of the six approaches earlier listed, just keep on preaching till it is evident through the blessing that comes to the sinners as well as through sensing your own inner feeling.

(6) Can the sixth approach mentioned in (3) above — namely, living faith — be used independently?

This sixth approach may be used together with all the other five approaches. Yet it can also be used independently as the result of seeing Jesus as the Friend of sinners.

(7) In helping those who preach the gospel by pointing out their weaknesses in the preaching, would this not increase their self-consciousness?

That is very true. Hence in helping them, be very careful not to increase their self-consiousness, or else they shall become inhibited.

(8) How about gospel resources?

The preaching of our Lord as recorded in the New Testament Gospels aims at moving people towards believing. The teachings or doctrines in the Epistles are to help people to know what they believe. As recorded in Luke 8. 4–8, our Lord spoke by means of a parable and closed with: "He that hath ears to hear, let him hear." These are words for drawing the gospel net, in that they cause people to incline towards what He has said. Whenever the word of our Lord was given, His Spirit was released. There seems to have been a law or principle to His speaking that was constantly in operation, for He always used words that struck at the heart.

Let us note the following examples of this: "Take heed therefore how ye hear: for whosoever hath, to him shall be given; and whosoever hath not, from him shall be taken away even that which he thinketh he hath" (Luke 8. 18); "Look therefore whether the light that is in thee be not darkness" (11. 35); "So is he that layeth up treasure for himself, and is not rich toward God" (12. 21); "Be ye also ready: for in an hour that ye think not the Son of man cometh" (12. 40); "And to whomsoever much is given, of him shall much be required: and to whom they commit much, of him will they ask the more" (12. 48b); "I say unto thee, Thou shalt by no means come out thence, till thou have paid the very last mite" (12. 59); "I tell you, Nay: but, except ye repent, ye shall all likewise perish" (13. 5). Whoever is preaching the gospel needs to use these gospel words which can touch the heart. Even those who sing must sing with the spirit of the gospel.

For the church to preach the gospel, there is need of oneness of spirit as a certain measure of prearrangement. The church must train the brothers and sisters in the preaching of the gospel. The responsible brothers should be faithful in supervising and encouraging brothers and sisters to bring in friends to hear the gospel. They themselves must set the example.

(9) How can we help those brethren who attend the gospel meeting?

First of all, any brother should be reminded that he should not measure the spirit of the meeting with his own spirit. Sometimes his own spirit is at a low ebb. The meeting may be good, but he is as an outsider. If he touches defilement in the meeting, then something is wrong in the meeting.

Secondly, in order to touch the spirit of other brethren, one has to deal strictly with himself first. Be very careful in learning how to touch others' spirit.

(10) How are we to prepare for the gospel beforehand and what about spontaneous inspiration?

There should be preparation beforehand. The introductory words need to be strong and impressive. In drawing the gospel net, the spirit should be free and spontaneous. One brother in England frequently used the sentence: "No one load can be placed on two backs." Brother M'Kendrick himself often declared: "You and hell are not far apart, just a breath's length."

(11) Sometimes when the word is uttered it draws out tears; but at other times, when the same word is spoken, there are no tears. Why is this?

The same word must be spoken with the same spirit in order to achieve the same result. Otherwise, you will have different responses.

(12) Does the "fire" in Matthew 3. 11c—"He shall baptize you in the Holy Spirit and in fire"—refer to the fire of the gospel?

No, the "fire" here refers to the fire of hell. As the "Holy Spirit" is to be taken literally, so must the "fire" be taken literally. This is an important principle of interpretation. The Lord uses the Holy Spirit to baptize the believers, whereas He uses fire to season the unbelievers.

(13) How many people should speak in an open-air meeting?

This is not a question of how many people should speak but rather a matter of how much time there is. If the time is long, several can speak. The messages must be concise and the prayers must be short.

(14) If a sinner prolongs his weeping, will he be exposed to demon possession?

The cry of repentance does not usually open the door to demon possession, unless that person has already been possessed by a demon.

(15) May we take those who weep naturally or supernaturally outside of the meeting to help them?

You may, but remember to never forbid normal weeping. Sheep usually go astray as a group and will also return as a group.

(16) How about this matter of hearing confession?

Never try to hear people's confession of sins. For confession is like a water ditch, and hearing confession is like a water reservoir. The knowledge of the sinning perpetrated by many Catholic priests has come about from their continual hearing of confession. Many revivalists have themselves fallen into sins because they have listened to confessions. Do not ever hear others' confession. The most one should do is to hear but the mentioning of sin, never to hear the story itself of the sin(s). How pure is our Lord who alone can hear the confession of all the repentant sinners and believers in the world and not be defiled. He knows no sin; He is the blessed Lord.

(17) How about the matter of demon possession?

One basic principle of demon possession is the breakdown of the walls of personality. Open confession of a believer tends to break down the walls of his personality. God alone examines our hearts and tries our reins (see Ps. 26. 2). We need to keep the fence of our personality intact. Failure to do so leads to fulfilling the condition for demon possession.

(18) How much time should be spent in drawing the net?

It is very difficult to calculate the time. Some people have to be pressed while others are averse to pressure. But if the church is under the mercy of the Lord, she will be blessed either way.

Part III

The Unsearchable Riches of the Gospel

A. GOD SEEKS MEN

> There is none that understandeth, there is none that seeketh after God; they have all turned aside, they are together become unprofitable; there is none that doeth good, no, not so much as one. (Rom 3. 11–12)
>
> For the Son of man came to seek and to save that which was lost. (Luke 19. 10)

We do praise and thank God, for it is not we who love God, but God has first loved us. According to Romans 3. 11–12, there is none who seeks after God. And in Luke 19. 10 we are told by the Lord Jesus himself that "the Son of man came to seek and to save that which was lost." We thank God because he has not commanded us, as He did the people of the Old Testament time, to approach Him by bringing sheep and bullocks with them. Instead, He has set His tabernacle among us through His own Son so that we may draw near to Him.

None of us dares to say that we seek after God and salvation on our own initiative. I have worked among unbelievers for some time, and I have yet to meet one who has himself sought God. Mr. Paget Wilkes said that he had preached to tens of thousands of people in Japan but had never met one person who sought after God.

There is none in the world who is for the Lord. Only the Lord is for men. This is indeed grace. This is the gospel. Do the idol-worshippers seek after God? No, they seek after their own welfare. Some hope for success in business, while some expect to have peace in the family. What they seek after is blessing. They seek not for God but for that which is God's. Yet what God seeks after are persons such as we are. What men look for are the grace, the peace, and the blessing of God. What God looks for are we ourselves, not what is ours. Let us break forth in praises and thanks before God today. How good God has treated us! It is something beyond our expectation!

"And this, not as we had hoped, but first they gave their own selves to the Lord, and to us through the will of God" (2 Cor. 8. 5). Do we notice here how God desires us? He is not greedy. Does He covet the wealth of the rich? No, He wants you and me. None seeks after God. What men expect are the peace and blessing of God. But God seeks us. Though no one seeks Him, God nonetheless seeks us.

Suppose God wants something from you. What can

you give Him? You and I have nothing at all to give. That which God looks for are men and women. It is well if a person is saved, for this is what God desires. Before you were saved, you lived in the world without the Savior. You had never thought of eternal life, nor did you ever think of the future destiny. You might have heard of God, but you wanted to have nothing to do with Him. You might even have hated Him without cause. Nonetheless, thank God, He has saved you! He loved you and me so much as to send His only begotten Son to the world to seek and save us. His Son gave up His life and shed His blood to redeem us.

We do not start out as the prodigal son. We begin as the lost sheep sought after first by the shepherd. In Luke 15, there are three parables: one concerning a shepherd who lost a sheep, who then went out to find it; another about a woman who lost one piece of silver, and who then swept the house to recover it; and a third that related the story of a father who received a repentant, prodigal son back home. Figuratively speaking, therefore, we see first, the Savior who came to seek you; next, the Holy Spirit who enlightens you; and finally, the Father who receives you back. Praise and thank God, He has sought us and saved us.

B. WHO CRUCIFIED THE LORD?

He was despised, and rejected of men; a man of sorrows, and acquainted with grief: and as one from whom men hide their face he was despised; and we esteemed him not. (Is. 53. 3)

The God of Abraham, and of Isaac, and of Jacob, the God of our fathers, hath glorified his Servant Jesus; whom ye delivered up, and denied before the face of Pilate, when he had determined to release him. But ye denied the Holy and Righteous One, and asked for a murderer to be granted unto you, and killed the Prince of life; whom God raised from the dead; whereof we are witnesses. And by faith in his name hath his name made this man strong, whom ye behold and know: yea, the faith which is through him hath given him this perfect soundness in the presence of you all. (Acts 3. 13–16)

And they that passed by railed on him, wagging their heads . . . In like manner also the chief priests mocking him, with the scribes and elders . . . And the robbers also that were crucified with him cast upon him the same reproach. Now from the sixth hour there was darkness over all the land until the ninth hour. And about the ninth hour Jesus cried with a loud voice, saying, Eli, Eli, lama sabachthani? that is, My God, my God, why hast thou forsaken me? . . . And Jesus cried again with a loud voice, and yielded up his spirit. And behold, the veil of the temple was rent in two from the top to the bottom; and the earth did quake; and the rocks were rent . . . (Matt. 27. 39–52)

Saying, Father, if thou be willing, remove this cup from me: nevertheless not my will, but thine, be done. (Luke 22. 42)

In Acts 8 we are told that Philip the Evangelist

pointed out to the eunuch that Isaiah 53.7-8, as quoted in Acts 8.32-33 — "He was led as a sheep to the slaughter; and as a lamb before his shearer is dumb, so he openeth not his mouth: in his humiliation his judgment was taken away: his generation who shall declare? For his life is taken from the earth" — referred to the death of Jesus Christ. In this same chapter of Isaiah, we are twice challenged with words such as: "he was wounded for our transgressions, he was bruised for our iniquities" (v.5) and ". . . who among them considered that he was cut off out of the land of the living for the transgression of my people to whom the stroke was due?" (v.8) In the eyes of men, Jesus must have died for His own sins because a person who obeys God and lives a holy life should never, and *would* never, encounter such malignancy. The Jews despise Him for this very reason. Here is One who was despised and punished for sin. Who in the world knew that He had borne their iniquities? He was smitten and His life violently taken away from Him. Who in the world ever considered that this was for *their* transgressions? How the world has mistaken His death as being for His own sins. Solomon once observed that "the way of the transgressor is hard" (Prov. 13. 15b). And hence Isaiah raised the challenge of who ever knew or considered otherwise?

We cannot explain the death of the Lord Jesus according to man's traditional way of thinking. God has put our sins upon Him as our substitute. He died because *God* caused Him to die. For God set Him forth to be a propitiation (Rom. 3. 25). Peter and John testified: "Jesus; whom ye delivered up, and denied before the face of Pilate, when he had determined to release him. But ye denied the Holy and righteous One,

. . . and killed the Prince of life." People are indeed so deranged as to have thought and said that Christ had died for His own sins. But Isaiah has made it clear that "it pleased Jehovah to bruise him" (53. 10). Peter looked at the cross from the human viewpoint; that is why he said, "[You] killed the Prince of life." There is another equally valid viewpoint, however, which is, that God had so ordered that it must be so. Hence Jesus was crucified by *God* as well as *men*.

Who condemned Jesus? During that time the religious authority of Judaism had no power to kill, though it had possessed such power prior to the Roman occupation. Since the fall of the nation, however, this power to kill had been taken away from them and rested in the Roman authority. As for Pilate, he had not considered it a crime for Jesus to have said that He was the *Son of God*. But he became alarmed when he heard that Jesus was *King*. Yet Jesus, unlike other political prisoners, made no defense. The Jews asked to crucify Him, and in the end the Roman soldiers themselves did the crucifying. Everything seemed to have been done by men. In the eyes of the world, He who had sinned must be crucified. If He were the Son of God and were sinless, God would surely defend Him.

So the soldiers mocked Jesus for three hours. But commencing from noon onward, God stepped in: "There was darkness over all the land till the ninth hour." This was something men could not do. God alone could do it. The sun was darkened, and in the holy temple the veil that was tens of feet tall was rent from top to bottom. This was not anything men could do because men could only rend such a very high veil from the bottom up instead of in the reverse direction. Neither could men cause the earthquake nor rend the rocks nor open the tombs. All these were done by God, not by men. There was therefore a considerable part in the death of Jesus that was played by God.

If the Lord's death were not a propitiatory death, He would not have died a good death. His death would have been inferior to the death of a martyr. A martyr in dying could declare: "Lord, I thank You for giving me the opportunity to testify to Your word with this body of mine." Yet our Lord sweat blood. His was a shameful death for He bore our sins in His body. How terrible He must have felt. One who had never touched sin bore the sin of the whole world.

A first-century Christian leader named Polycarp was arrested. The proconsul urged him to swear by the genius of Caesar and say, "Away with the atheists." He caught up the last words of his judge. With solemn visage, and looking up to heaven and waving his hand, Polycarp cried out: "Away with the atheists." The proconsul, perhaps mistaking this as a sign of yielding and recanting his Christian faith, pressed him further: "Swear, and I will set thee free; revile Christ." His answer is memorable: "Four-score and six years have I served Him, and He hath done me no wrong. How then can I speak evil of my King, who saved me?" All threats and seductions alike having proved powerless, the proconsul announced to the assembled multitude that Polycarp had confessed himself a Christian. Whereupon the pyre was readied and heaped up. There he offered up his last prayer—words of praise and thanksgiving that God had deigned to accept him that day as a sacrifice well-pleasing to Him.

Yet in the case of our Lord Jesus, He cried out, "My God, my God, why hast thou forsaken me?" If His death had not been for the atoning of sin, it would have been far inferior to Polycarp's death. Yes, Polycarp died to testify, but our Lord died to atone. From eternity to eternity, He is the Savior. God had never before separated Himself from His Son. Only when His Son was made sin for us did God forsake Him. Where there is sin, there can be no light. Surely in God's eye, His Son is indeed the Redeemer of sinful men.

On the cross, our Lord spoke seven words, which were: (1) "Father, forgive them; for they know not what they do" — forgive on the basis of atonement; (2) "Today shalt thou be with me in Paradise" — the teaching out of redemption; (3) "Behold, thy mother," Jesus had said to John — signifying that all who are born of God become one family, and this is due to the work of redemption; (4) "My God, my God, why hast thou forsaken me?" — He who knew no sin was made sin for us; (5) "I thirst" — for the wrath of God was on Him; (6) "It is finished" — He cried with a loud voice that it was done, indicating by this that the work of redemption was finished; and (7) "Father, into thy hands I commend my spirit" — He gave up or dismissed his spirit, which meant that though men could crucify Him they themselves could not put Him to death. He himself gave up His own life.

The veil is now rent; otherwise, no man could ever draw near to God. Man of old could enter into the holy place, but never the holiest of all except for the high priest who in type represented the Great High Priest

(Jesus) who was to come. It is God who has rent the veil; thus the way to God is opened. Because Christ died, I now can live. Because He lives, I may enter into glory.

C. OUR LORD ALWAYS MINISTERS

The Son of man also came not to be ministered unto, but to minister, and to give his life a ransom for many. (Mark 10. 45)

But ye shall not be so: but he that is the greater among you, let him become as the younger; and he that is chief, as he that doth serve. For which is greater, he that sitteth at meat, or he that serveth? is not he that sitteth at meat? but I am in the midst of you as he that serveth. (Luke 22. 26–27)

Blessed are those servants, whom the Lord when he cometh shall find watching: verily I say unto you, that he shall gird himself, and make them sit down to meat, and shall come and serve them. (Luke 12. 37)

These three Scripture portions show us how Christ ministers to us in the past, in the present, and in the future.

Let us look at the first Scripture: "the Son of man

also came not to be ministered unto, but to minister, and to give his life a ransom for many." This verse tells us that the Son of man came to serve all men. Whoever came to Him, He would serve that one. He gave food to the hungry; He healed the sick. He served any person at any time at any place. His highest service lay in giving His life as a ransom for many. He served with His life. Oftentimes, we today are thinking how we may serve God. Do we really know that on the cross Christ served us with His own life? When we were yet sinners, He had served us.

Now turn to the second passage: "But ye shall not be so: but he that is the greater among you, let him become as the younger; and he that is chief, as he that doth serve. For which is greater, he that sitteth at meat, or he that serveth? is not he that sitteth at meat? But I am in the midst of you as he that serveth." Mark told us in the first passage of how Christ served the sinners; here, Luke speaks to us of how Christ serves the disciples. "I am in the midst of you," Jesus said, "as he that serveth." Let us always remember that Christ in our midst is now serving us. This is grace!

The bread that is before us at the Lord's Table indicates the way Christ serves us today. His body is broken for our sake. Before we can ever serve Christ, He first serves us. This is salvation. He serves us not only on Calvary's cross but also in our very midst. Whenever we have need, let us go to Him and let Him serve us.

Once after He sent the multitude away, Jesus went alone to the mountain to pray. Below Him His disciples were in a boat. They were distressed in rowing, for the wind was quite contrary to them. About the fourth watch of the night, which is the darkest hour as well as the sleepiest time, the Lord came to their rescue. They, however, thought it was a ghost and cried out with fear. But He straightway spoke to them, "Be of good cheer: it is I; be not afraid" (see Mark 6. 45-51). He could have said to them, "It is your Lord" or "It is the Son of God"; yet He simply said, "It is I." What does this mean? Suppose someone knocks at the door, then the person inside asks who is there, and the one who did the knocking replies, "It is I." This would imply that he is an acquaintance of the person inside, so the latter will recognize his voice. When our Lord came to the aid of His disciples, He came to help and identified himself in the most intimate way. Since this is so, how we ought to enjoy the service of Christ to us today!

Let us recall how the Lord had had no need to pay the tribute money. And even if He had *had* to do so, He would have needed only to pay half a shekel. Yet He was mindful of Peter's need; so He asked Peter to go cast a hook into the sea, and in the mouth of the first fish caught there would be a shekel, enough to pay for both His *and* Peter's tribute money. How He served Peter by prearrangement! (see Matt. 17. 24-27)

As we read through the four Gospels, can we not see the Lord serving His disciples again and again? We will be surprised, for we would think that Christ's followers should serve Him but never expect that Christ should serve them. Why does the Lord serve His own? Jesus first explains man's view of the situation: "Which is greater, he that sitteth at meat, or he that serveth? is not he that sitteth at meat?" But our Lord then went on to say: "I am in the midst of you as he that serveth." For *He* is the greater, yea, He is the greatest; therefore He serves. So that the divine view is that the greater a person is, the more he is able to serve; the smaller a person is, the less he can serve. The smallest probably may serve no one. Our Lord is great, and His greatness is without limit. For this reason, He can serve men without end.

"I am the light of the world," the Lord declared (John 8. 12a). What else may serve mankind more than light? He who follows the light shall not walk in darkness, but shall have the light of life. "I am the bread of life," the Lord declared as well. What may serve mankind more than food? He who eats this bread shall live forever. Indeed, whatever our Lord does, it is to serve man. Hallelujah, we have a Lord who serves us! In time of distress or helplessness, we give Him opportunity to serve us. He is great, so great that He is able to serve us in all things.

On still another occasion, the Lord washed the feet of His disciples. According to Peter, this was something "never" to be done. Yet the Lord washed their feet and served them (see John 13. 4-8).

Finally, when people came to seize Him, the Lord asked them whom they sought. They answered Him, "Jesus of Nazareth." Jesus said, "I told you that I am he; if therefore ye seek me, let these [His disciples] go their way" (John 18. 8). How mindful was our Lord of His disciples. From beginning to end, the Lord served them.

And at the very end, the Lord had spoken to the Father in this way: "Of those whom thou hast given me I lost not one" (John 18.9). How true it is that the Lord will serve us from the first day till the last.

There is yet a third passage that was quoted above: "Blessed are those servants, whom the Lord when he cometh shall find watching: verily I say unto you, that he shall gird himself, and make them sit down to meat, and shall come and serve them." What kind of grace this is! How could such a thing be? But the Lord says He shall yet serve us. We who once owed Him much receive grace freely. Now we owe Him eternally, and therefore we enjoy grace eternally.

I wonder how many of us today know how to enjoy the service of Christ. Most of the time we have the wrong idea that it is we who should serve Christ. Do we desire His serving us? Someone says his prayer is so cold, and so he tries to work up zeal. He should know that Christ will serve him at this very time for this very need. Someone else thinks that he does not know how to read the Bible; therefore, he plans to study it differently tomorrow. Does he not realize that Christ is able to serve here as well?

God gives us Christ that He may serve us. From His death on the cross to eternity future, Christ is serving us. Though this is beyond our comprehension, we can still enjoy. Do not refuse as Peter did, but lean instead on the Lord's breast as John did.

D. PRESENT THE BODIES

> I beseech you therefore, brethren, by the mercies of God, to present your bodies a living sacrifice, holy, acceptable to God, which is your spiritual service. (Rom. 12. 1)

Here we find the apostle "beseech[ing]" the believers to present their bodies. He *could* have *ordered* them, but he would rather beseech, since this is something that must be carried out willingly; otherwise, it is useless. Let us note, however, that he does not ask them to present their spirits or their souls, but only their bodies. Why is this so? Here we can see the important position the body occupies. To present the body is something "acceptable to God." Although God does not communicate directly with man through the body, but takes the spirit as His dwelling place, He nonetheless does not despise man's body. The spirit occupies the first place, but the body has its rightful position too.

Without doubt, a man ought to let the Holy Spirit have the preeminence in whatever he does; nevertheless, this does not mean that he can neglect the body. Once we have seen how God emphasizes the intuition, communion and conscience of the human spirit, we are tempted to fall prey easily to imagining that God does not care about the body, that the body has no other function than to hurt us, and that if our life in the spirit is strong and full of power we can totally ignore this outward vessel. However, God's view is quite different. Though He does stress the life in the spirit, He nonetheless affirms that the salvation provided by His Son must reach to this outward vessel as well. Salvation is less than effective if it fails to touch the body.

Furthermore, the presenting of the body is in actuality the presenting of *all* because the body here represents the whole being. Since the believer's spirit has already become attuned to God, it has no need to be offered up again. On the other hand, his soul and body are not yet in perfect harmony with the life of God, and hence must be offered up. Though only the body is mentioned here, it actually includes the soul, for our present body is closely knit with the soul. The Bible calls it "a natural body," 1 Corinthians 15. 44 in the original terming it a "psychical" or "soulical body." Thus, in presenting the body, a person presents all that he *naturally* possesses. We notice here that God's purpose is not confined to just our inward man, it also includes our outward man. It is true that in this matter of communion with God, the outward man is absolutely useless, since such communion is carried on in the inward man. Nevertheless, in other matters the importance of the outward man cannot be overlooked; else the Holy Spirit would not have issued here such a call for it to be offered up.

What is really meant by presenting the body? It means to live for the Lord as well as to work for the Lord. To understand this, we must know what the body is. It is very different from the spirit in one area; that is to say, the body is bound by time and place whereas the spirit is not. The body is outside, so it has a special relationship to outward things. In presenting the body, we naturally offer up time and place and every contact with the natural world. Hence, it means nothing less than to live and work for the Lord.

Now of these two aspects, to *live* for the Lord is more primary. Many consider working for the Lord as living for the Lord, not recognizing there is a vast difference between the two. People are able to work for the Lord and still not live for Him; whereas all who live for the Lord will work for Him too. To live for the Lord signifies that not a single moment is reserved for self-seeking, but that a believer's entire time is given to the Lord (though not necessarily working for the Lord). The Holy Spirit is now calling believers to present their bodies in order to live for the Lord.

Now let us look at the entire verse, portion by portion. "Brethren"—this is spoken to believers. "By the mercies of God"—presenting the body is due to the mercies of God. It is because of all the gracious dealings and love of God that the body will be presented. This agrees with the words of 2 Corinthians 5. 14–15: "the love of Christ constrains us; . . . that they that live should no longer live unto themselves, but unto him who for their sakes died and rose again." What is this presenting the body for? As "a living sacrifice." A sacrifice is usually dead, but God wants our bodies to be a *living* sacrifice. In the Old Testament time, the bodies of the sacrifices were laid on the altar slain. Today God calls us to present our bodies alive to Him as a sacrifice. This denotes our living as though dead. As long as we shall live on earth, we present ourselves as sacrifices already dead. And this kind of sacrifice is "holy, acceptable to God." Due to the mercies of God, this is our "spiritual service."

Let us see that God has already secured His place *within* us, now He asks us to present the *outward* to Him. He has already begun to dwell in our spirit, in our inward man. He now waits for us to present our bodies—our outward man—to Him too. Since we live *by* Him, He expects us to live *for* Him. The spirit being renewed, our tabernacles of flesh should also be wholly committed to God. Thus this renewed spirit will have a willing body to cooperate with it in living and working for God. And this is God's good pleasure.

E. TRUST AND OBEY

Even so reckon ye also yourselves to be dead unto sin but alive unto God in Christ Jesus. Let not sin therefore reign in your mortal body, that ye should obey the lusts thereof: neither present your members unto sin as instruments of unrighteousness; but present yourselves unto God, as alive from the dead, and your members as instruments of righteousness unto God. For sin shall not have dominion over you: for ye are not under law, but under grace. (Rom. 6. 11–14)

Today I would speak on the principles of Christian

living. What the entire New Testament shows us is that there are only two principles of Christian living, with all the rest that pertains to the believer's life constituting the fruits of these two principles. Whether that fruit be patience or gentleness or faithfulness or self-control, these are not themselves to be taken as principles of Christian living. For there are actually but two basic ones to be considered: the one is to trust, the other is to obey. All good fruits in our Christian lives flow from these two fundamental axioms. In our daily walk with the Lord, we need to trust and obey.

There are many places in the New Testament which speak of trust and obey. It will suffice us here to focus only on the eleventh and thirteenth verses of Romans 6. The verb "reckon" in verse 11 conveys the idea of "trust"; whereas the verb "present" (or "yield"—Darby's translation) in verse 13 conveys the idea of "obey." The "trust" element in verse 11 is in connection with the finished work of Christ; the "obey" element in verse 13, on the other hand, challenges us to maintain the position of faith and trust we have obtained. By keeping the balance between trust and obey, we may freely enter into all the spiritual experiences reserved for us.

How should we explain this dual principle of "trust and obey"? All the *objective* truths are in Christ; and all which is in Christ has *already* been accomplished. All the *subjective* truths are in the Holy Spirit; and all which is in the Holy Spirit *awaits to be fulfilled* by the Holy Spirit. In this connection, I wonder if we believers know the difference between redemption and salvation. The first is that which was accomplished over nineteen hundred years ago, but the second is that which is fulfilled on the day we believe in the Lord and thereafter. Hence redemption is objective in nature—that which has been accomplished in Christ; salvation, on the other hand, is subjective in nature—that which is to be wrought in us continually by the Holy Spirit. These two are irreversible. The Lord Jesus did not finish salvation about two thousand years ago nor does He accomplish redemption in His people day by day currently. No, redemption was accomplished long ago, whereas salvation is continually waiting to be fulfilled.

Suppose I am unsaved, and you are preaching the gospel to me. You can only say to me that the work of *redemption* has been finished, you cannot say the work of *salvation* has been completed, because I am not yet saved. Salvation is fulfilled after I believe in the Lord, whereas redemption has long since been accomplished. All the works of redemption belong in the past, because all the objective works have been done absolutely and limitlessly. But all the subjective works must be wrought now and on into the future. And hence we can say that the one is already done, the other remains to be done. On the one side were the death, burial, resurrection and ascension of our Lord. On the other side, though, the Holy Spirit will take this death spoken of here and put it in you once you believe. In the same way, too, the resurrection of Christ spoken of here happened once nineteen hundred years ago, but its manifestation in you occurs on the day you believe. All the objective elements are past, absolute and complete, with nothing able to be added. But all the subjective aspects are to be achieved now and hereafter.

For this reason, the ways of accepting objective and

subjective truths are totally different from each other. On the one hand, since the objective has already been accomplished, it needs to be believed or trusted in. On the other hand, since the subjective awaits to be achieved now and in the future, it should be obeyed or yielded to. Any attention paid to one side only will result in the believer being lost either in presumption or in dead works. The objective truths of death, burial, resurrection and ascension require faith. But faith alone is not enough, for day by day these truths demand obedience. Co-death calls for yieldedness. The power of resurrection and the position of ascension bid obedience.

We who have become Christians need the Savior on both the inside and the outside. We need the Word manifested in the Holy Spirit as well as the Word manifested in the flesh. We need the Christ of Golgotha, to be sure, but we also need the Christ in the Spirit. As to the crucified, resurrected and ascended Christ outside of us, we must believe; as to the Spirit of Christ within us we must obey. Let me illustrate with some particular experiences in order to help us understand what is meant by "trust and obey."

What is meant by the first element, "trust"? Never a day can we be lax in the objective truths. It is not as man says, that I *shall* die, *shall* be raised from the dead and *shall* ascend to heaven; for the *facts* are that I have *already* died, *already* been resurrected and have *already* ascended — in Christ. What is faith? Faith or trust or believing is a knowing, seeing and reckoning. Who can believe what he has not seen? Be it death or resurrection or ascension, it requires the revelation of the Holy Spirit to generate faith. Doctrinal speaking is a mere talking about a thing, but truth presents the reality behind the word. Oftentimes doctrines are not truths, because truths include realities as well as words. The words "Christ died for us" do not convey a mere doctrine; they also convey a reality. What is taught in theology is doctrine. In other words, doctrine is theology. Objective truths, though, demand our faith. We must *know* deep within us that they are true. Truth, in Greek, means reality. The death of Christ is truth because His death is real. His resurrection is truth, which again means that His resurrection is factual and real. His ascension likewise is truth, for His ascension is that which is true, factual and real. This is what is meant by truth.

How do we know these are truths? Each time we accept a truth, it is not because the preacher says so. In the entire universe there is only One who can lead us into truth, and He is the Holy Spirit. A preacher can only preach the doctrine, but the Holy Spirit can reveal the truth for us to believe. Do we see this? I will not speak today about our co-death, co-resurrection, and co-ascension with Christ; I will simply speak on this matter of Christ having died for us.

Formerly you neither knew sin nor God nor Christ. Perhaps one day you heard people talking about the substitutionary death of Christ, and that word touched your heart. You then say to yourself, "What has happened?" The answer is that you "saw" your sins; you "saw" Christ. In a word, you "saw" salvation. You saw that your sins were forgiven, and dared to say that your sins were indeed forgiven. If people were to ask you how you know your sins are forgiven, you would be very sure because you have *seen*.

What is the revelation of the Holy Spirit? It is the Holy Spirit opening the veil, as it were, to let you see the substance or reality behind the word of the preacher. You see what forgiveness is and what regeneration is. This seeing is most valuable. You see that Jesus Christ died for you, therefore you can believe.

Let us assume that you go to the country to preach to your longtime friend. He nods his head while you talk, but he shortly thereafter forgets all you have said. He lacks one thing, which is, that he has not received revelation. His eyes are still blind, so he cannot believe. Quite simply stated: no revelation, no faith. You should ask God to cause your friend to see his sins and see the Savior. Then you do not need to give him many doctrines. Death calls for seeing. Burial calls for seeing. Any truth, including also resurrection or ascension, requires a seeing.

Let us say that you go to the village and preach the gospel to fifty people. You tell them how men have sinned, how the Lord died for them; and that believing, they will be saved. They all nod their approval, but are they all saved? In spite of showing their approval, they go away without any sense of guilt about lying or pride. They have *heard* of sins, but they have not *seen* sins. They have *heard* of the Savior, but they have not *seen* the Savior; therefore, they do not have the ability to *believe*. Each time we preach the gospel, we must ask God to open people's eyes that they may weep for their sins and cannot help but accept the Savior. And if such happens, then later on, even were a doctor of liberal theology to attempt to dissuade them otherwise by saying that their sins are nothing and Christ's death was merely exemplary in nature, they will not be shaken. For they have seen; and therefore, they can believe and have believed.

Death is an objective truth that calls for faith. All the objective truths require the element of faith. We lay much stress on the Lord's death when we preach. Yet why does this not have the proper effect? It is because something is wrong in the area of faith, which means something is wrong with revelation. Once I spoke on the truth of co-death. A brother then said, "All is well now. Henceforth I am certain of victory, for I know the method of victory." I said to him, "This will lose its effectiveness after only a few days because you have not *seen* it."

If you ask a person how he got saved, and his reply is that he heard the doctrine, you know that this will fade away after but a few days. Mental understanding is not faith. As you open the Bible and read, or as you hear in the meeting that you have died, have been raised and have ascended, you should not look within yourself where you can see nothing of resurrection and ascension *in you*; neither should you carelessly claim that you have already died, been raised and have ascended. What you should do is to ask the Lord to cause you to *see* that you have indeed died, been raised and have ascended. By thus praying, you will be brought by the Lord into the objective truths, that is to say, you will be brought into the Lord himself and see that *in Christ only* have you died; because He was raised, you also were raised; because He ascended, you too have ascended. Then will you be able to say, "Lord, I thank You, for in You I have died, been raised and have ascended." You speak out of faith. And this faith is in the *fact* behind the word you have read or heard.

Mr. Hudson Taylor, the famed missionary to China, found himself continuously weak and defeated. Once he wrote to his sister confessing that his mind was in distress because he felt the inner lack of more holiness, life and power. He thought all would be well if he could abide in Christ. Naturally his sister prayed for him. He spent several months in prayer, struggle, fasting, making resolutions, searching the Scriptures, and meditating—yet all to no avail. How he longed to dwell forever in Christ, but he slipped out of Christ constantly. He acknowledged that all would be well if he could only abide in Christ, yet this he could not do.

In his diary Mr. Taylor wrote, in so many words, as follows: One day I was again praying. I thought if I could abide in Christ and draw from His sap and obtain His nutrition and supply, then I would have power to overcome sins. Again I prayed and read the Scriptures. When I came to John 15. 5 ("I am the vine, ye are the branches") I said to myself, "I am the most foolish person in the whole world! I have been praying that I might be a branch and abide in Christ. But the Lord says, 'You are *already* a branch, and you are *already* in Me.' "

If only we would understand this, we would shout Hallelujah! Let us see that we do not need to enter, because we are *already* in. Let us not try hard to *be* branches, nor to *become* branches after overcoming sins. Let us see that we *are* the branches; we are *already* in. The purpose of John 15. 5 is to tell us that we are already in; hence let us be careful not to slip out. And if we *are* the branches, the sap, the nutrition and love are therefore all ours. Mr. Taylor testified that after he saw and understood this truth, he became a new Hudson Taylor. This was one of the greatest crises in his entire Christian life.

Believing does not transform God's word into fact; no, it is believing in the *fact* of God's word. The grace of God includes three things: these are promise, fact and covenant. Concentrating today on the first two, we may say that promise will be fulfilled in the future, whereas fact is something already accomplished. All the objective truths are facts accomplished.

Many ask for death, but God says you are *already* dead in Christ. Many ask for resurrection and ascension, but God says that in Christ you have been raised and have ascended *already*. Many ask for victory over the world, yet the word of God says, "who is he that overcometh the world, but he that believeth . . ." (1 John 5. 5). All these are right there *in Christ*. We need seeing before we can believe. If any brother or sister sees the objective truth in just one verse of the Scriptures, he or she is able to believe and to walk onward.

Yet how many ask blindly. Have you ever heard a sinner asking Christ to die for him? Once while preaching the gospel, I heard such a one praying in this way: "O Lord, I am a sinner, please die for me." This is truly a wrong prayer. Is it not a joke for people to ask the Lord to die for them or to let them die with Him? How utterly futile is our brain. We must believe the word of God more than our circumstances, our feelings, our trials, our sins, our lusts and our unclean thoughts. Then we shall see the difference. It is not enough merely to hear; we must have the eye of faith. May we see all that God has accomplished in Christ already.

Even so, we should also understand that faith alone is still incomplete. It must be followed by *obedience*. We must believe on the one hand but obey on the other as well. We must lay aside our own ideas and present every member of our body to God. After we have come into living faith, we should learn to obey God day by day. Whenever a spot in us is touched by God, and we ask *Him* to yield to *us*, we have obviously not obeyed Him. Without the yielding of the will to God there can be no faith in Him. If a sinner is unwilling to repent, he cannot believe. If a believer embraces disobedience in his heart, neither can he trust.

In this matter of obedience many have a great deal of reservations about their families. Some are not willing to offer up their children. Some have an improper attitude towards their husbands. Some lack rightful distribution of money. Have you presented yourself to God? Are you willing to go wherever He sends you? Are you ready to perform the lowest duty He asks you to do? Believing alone may not maintain you in the finishing of your course. Perhaps as soon as you believe, God will ask you to obey. Or He may wait a while after you have believed before He asks you to obey. With some, He demands obedience before He gives faith. With others, He gives faith and then He requires obedience. He may even ask still others to obey at the same time He gives faith.

I do not know what God will require of each individual. I am certain, however, that having only one side of this dual principle leaves many things to be desired. Whoever considers faith alone to be enough, without presenting his body to God, is like a cake in an oven unturned (cf. Hosea 7. 8). Let us realize that we must yield to God. This special step must be taken. It is like crossing a threshold. In order for a person to be a steward in God's house, he must have a definite beginning. He must offer himself to God at a certain point. At one specific moment he must say to God that henceforth all his time, all his brain power, all his money, his family and his everything belong to God. During that time, God may touch him at a specific spot. This, of course, will vary from person to person. Oftentimes God's demand may seem a bit strict or harsh. Nevertheless, what He demands must be obeyed. This is because God wants to test you as to whether you will really listen to Him. Nothing is more precious to Him than an Isaac in a person's life. Yet the matter is not settled with mere lip consent. The Isaac in your life must literally be offered up before you will see God's "provided ram" (see Genesis 22. 13). Not till you have fully obeyed will God be satisfied. We each must cross this threshold in a most singular way.

We have an American friend who had once been to China. The story of his faith is indeed marvelous. The account of how the Lord has led him is as follows: He had already obtained a master's degree, and he was next studying for his doctor's degree. He was serving as a pastor on the one hand and studying philosophy on the other. But he sensed his weak spiritual life. So he prayed to God and confessed that he had many unbeliefs and many defeats in his walk. For two weeks, he prayed especially, asking God to fill him with the Holy Spirit that he might experience the victorious life and power as spoken of in the Scriptures.

In response God spoke to him as follows: "Do you really want what you ask for? If that is true, then you should not take the doctor's examination two months from now. For I have no need of a doctor of philosophy." He was troubled. The doctor's degree was almost in his grasp, and it would be a pity not to achieve it. So he knelt down to pray and negotiate with the Lord, he asking why the Lord did not allow him to be a doctor of philosophy as well as a pastor. One thing here may amaze us, however, which is, that God never negotiates with man. What He has asked, He has asked. Whatever He commands, He never changes.

These two months were most painful for our American friend. On the last Saturday before the examination was to be taken, the battle became especially fierce. To be a doctor of philosophy or to be filled with the Holy Spirit? Which was better—a doctorate degree or the victorious life? But, he argued, if others could have the doctor's degree and be used of God, why could he not? He struggled and argued and battled, but all was of no avail. How lovely to be a doctor of philosophy, but how equally lovely to be filled with the Holy Spirit! Yet God did not give in. It must be either the doctor of philosophy without the spiritual life or the spiritual life without the doctor of philosophy. Finally, with tears, he told God: "I yield. Though I have studied for the doctor's degree for two years now, and even though I have longed to be a doctor for over thirty years ever since my childhood, nevertheless, today, for the sake of obedience, I give it up." Whereupon he wrote a letter to the school authorities informing them he would not be taking the examination on the following Monday. He gave up the doctor of philosophy forever.

That night he was very tired. On the next day he must preach, but he had no sermon to give. So, he related to his audience the story of his obedience in a very simple and humble way. That morning three-fourths of the congregation wept and were revived. And he received the power from on high. He confessed later that had he known the consequence, he would have yielded earlier.

No one who is ever used of God has failed to cross this threshold of obedience. Do not anticipate making spiritual advance if you never expect to cross the threshold. People must obey as well as believe—and not just yield *once* in obedience, but yield always. Obedience without faith lacks power; but faith without obedience remains mere theory. Please remember always that the principles of living to be found in the Scriptures are basically the twin elements of trust and obey. It cannot be trust and not obey; nor can it be obey and not trust. To trust without obedience is false; and to obey without trusting is asceticism. In the church of God today, there is either a deficiency in faith or a deficiency in obedience. Indeed, all failures in the house of God can be traced ultimately to a deficiency in either one or both of these basic life principles of the spiritual walk.

By trusting and obeying we shall have eternal spring and perfect day: "the path of the righteous is as the dawning light, that shineth more and more unto the perfect day" (Prov. 4.18). May God bless us that we may walk perfectly before Him by being those who trust and obey.

F. LET THE WORD OF CHRIST DWELL IN YOU RICHLY

> Let the word of Christ dwell in you richly; in all wisdom teaching and admonishing one another with psalms and hymns and spiritual songs, singing with grace in your hearts to God. (Col. 3. 16)

Many among God's children are spiritually poor because they fail to have the word of God dwelling in their hearts richly according to the letter to the Colossians. Poverty in the word of God is the primary reason for, or constitutes the first step toward, spiritual poverty. A person who is poor before God may turn the pages of the Bible and read them, but he fails to touch what God's word is saying. He has no contact with God, and does not find life. This is why he is spiritually poor.

One

There was once a brother who had believed in the Lord for one year and had also been baptized. One day he met an older brother who asked him three questions he had great difficulty in answering.

The first question he was asked was: "You have believed in the Lord for over one year; have you read the Bible from page to page once?" The younger brother thought this was indeed a very hard question. For had he simply been asked, "Have you read the Bible?", he could easily have answered, since he did read the Bible every day. Furthermore, had he been asked, "How much time do you spend in reading the Bible?", he could have readily answered that question, too, for he spent quite some time in reading the Bible. But to be asked, "Have you read the Bible through once?", he could not answer in the affirmative. So he merely replied, "I read the Bible daily." But the older brother was wise and said, "I do not ask if you read the Bible every day. What I ask is whether you have finished reading the Bible from cover to cover once?" Finding no way of escape, the younger believer had to say, "I do read the Bible daily, but I have not read through it once." "You have believed in the Lord for over a year, yet you have not read the Bible through once?" During those few minutes, none of them could say anything more. But this young brother did say in his heart, "O Lord, if You give me another year, I am determined to read the Bible through at least once."

The older brother did not let him off, however, but continued by asking him a second question: "You have

been a Christian for more than a year; do you pray?"
"I pray daily, and I spend the entire afternoon on Satur-
days in prayer on the mountain," replied the young
brother. "Well, now, you have indeed prayed that much,"
responded the older brother; "but how many times has
God *answered* your prayers? Recall if you have had a
single distinct answer to prayer among your many prayers." The young believer thought for a while and found
himself embarrassed, because though he prayed a great
deal, he could not single out any prayer that had been
answered. "Maybe none," was his confession. "What!
You have been a Christian for more than a year, and
yet God has not answered your prayers once?"

This was followed by a third question: "You have
been a Christian now for over a year; have you led anyone to Christ? Do you know clearly that that person
came to the Lord because you preached the gospel to
him?" He pondered that he had actually preached the
gospel, but to say that anyone had clearly come to the
Lord through him would not be true; for although one
person might have appeared to have been saved through
him, he dare not claim it. So, again, he said, "None."
The older brother asked no more questions, but only
sighed and said, "Having believed in the Lord for over
one year, you have neither read the Bible through once,
nor received one answer to prayer, nor led any person
to Christ. What a pity!" At that very moment, this
young brother decided in his heart, "Lord, within this
year I will lead at least one person to Christ, have at
least one definite answer to prayer, and read the Bible
through at least once."

Thereafter, this brother had a new beginning. He

was determined to read the Bible from the beginning to the end. He counted the number of books and chapters in the Old and New Testaments, and arranged his time in such a way that he planned to read the Old Testament three times and the New Testament twelve to fourteen times within the year. Thank God, by the end of the year, God had enabled him to read even more than he had planned. From that year onward, he always took care to read the Bible well and much.

We want to ask especially the young brothers and sisters: How much of God's word do you read daily? Have you read the Bible through once? It is very easy for us in our spiritual pursuit to aim at a higher level and neglect the basic lessons. If you read the Bible at random and have not read it through once, we would advise you to change your way of reading. You should plan carefully how you will read the Bible. You should set apart a certain time each day and read the Bible carefully from cover to cover. Reading any book casually will reap very little. How much more ought we to read the Bible diligently from the beginning to the end, from Genesis to Malachi, from Matthew to Revelation. You must follow a plan; otherwise, even after ten years you will still be very poor in the word of God.

Two

There are many ways to read the Bible. Reading book by book from the beginning to the end is the most elementary way. There is another method which a Christian should put into practice at the very start of his Christian life. He should rise up early in the morning to read the Bible. A prerequisite for such reading is to get up early. Only those who are physically ill and advised by physicians to rest more are an exception. Otherwise, all healthy people should rise a little earlier. For when the sun is hot, the manna vanishes (see Ex. 16. 21). Many fail in their Bible reading because they read the word at too late an hour. Let us take advantage of the dawn to carefully read God's word.

Even so, none can rise early if he goes to sleep late. The exceptions are those with night duties. Yet some people have no reason to stay up late, but due to habit they like to postpone things and do them at night. Since they go to sleep late, naturally they cannot get up early in the morning. There are also people who have nothing to do; they simply like to linger in the evening and pass their time in small talk. Such people who waste their time in this way and are unskillful in arranging a schedule can hardly rise up early and do things systematically. Let us cultivate the habit of going to sleep on time and rising on time. In this matter of early rising, many reveal their weakness and lack of self-control. They are not able to rise early to meet with God. Young Christians especially should develop this habit of early rising as soon as possible. The first day one may need a little push; the second and the third days may not be too difficult; gradually it will become natural and habitual.

One brother decided at first to rise up each morning between 4:30 and 5:00 a.m. When he woke up the first day, it was already 6:00 o'clock. The second day he again woke up at six. He was determined to rise at five in the morning. That night he did not sleep well, for intermittently he looked at his watch all the time. He realized that this would never work. How could he get up early if he could not sleep at night? He knew he could only trust God. So, on the third evening, he prayed, "God, I am now going to sleep. I put myself in Your hand that You will wake me up at five." That night he slept with confidence. As he woke up the next morning, he was quite alarmed that it might be six o'clock. But, thank God, it was five o'clock sharp. From that day onward, he was able to wake up on time. We believe God will wake us up if we truly trust Him.

We are not persuading everyone to rise at five. It may be good for some to get up even a little earlier than five, or for others to rise a little later than five. We do not advocate extremes. Each must decide before God according to his or her physical strength. You should figure out how many hours you need to sleep each night and then plan for the time to go to bed and to rise out of bed. You may get up at five or half past five or even at six. This you must arrange carefully before God. With such an arrangement, you will be able to read the word of God each morning.

We can testify that the Scripture you read in the presence of God in the early morning is the best nourishment you will ever receive for your spiritual life. You may read the Bible at other times, but reading in the early morning has a special flavor and benefit about it. If there is anyone here who has not been benefited by early morning reading, we hope that person will exercise himself to receive such blessing.

Three

"Let the word of Christ dwell in you richly." To let the word dwell in the heart is more than memorizing; it is something to be taken to heart. Our Lord teaches us to pray, "Give us this day our daily bread" (Matt. 6. 11). We should in truth pray for our daily bread. Yet "man shall not live by bread alone, but by every word that proceedeth out of the mouth of God" (Matt. 4. 4). Hence we need to ask God for our spiritual food as well as for our physical food. We need to ask Him to teach us how to take His word into our hearts.

Reading the Bible in the early morning should not be done as is done in ordinary reading—that is to say, you should not just keep reading on. You should instead meditate and pray as you read. After you have read a verse or two, or a sentence or two, you should start praying. Do not keep on reading, but mix your prayer with the word you read. Such prayer also differs from ordinary prayer that is offered up and ends with, "In the name of the Lord Jesus, Amen." On the contrary, as you read the word of God from the Bible you speak to God in your prayer. You place God's word before Him, and you read it to God as well as yourself. You pray as you read. Do not read quickly, but slowly chew the word. Thus shall you receive nourishment from the Bible.

For example, let us say you are reading Isaiah 54. 1, which says: "Sing, O barren, thou that didst not bear; break forth into singing, and cry aloud, thou that didst not travail with child: for more are the children of the desolate than the children of the married wife, saith

Jehovah." This tells us that what man does not have according to the flesh the Lord is able to give by the Spirit. As you read it, you meditate. Then you say to the Lord, "Lord, I neither bear nor travail with child; I have nothing to offer people in spiritual things. But I thank You, and I praise You; You are able to give to me because You have the power."

Whatever passage in the Scriptures you read, you should meditate and pray. Someone may say he is short of prayer topics; actually, in the Bible there are *plenty* of subjects for prayer. Wherever you read, you find topics for prayer. There is so much in the Bible that causes you to pray, to praise, to confess and to intercede.

Suppose you read a commandment of God out of His word. You will perhaps say to God: "God, forgive my sin, for I am weak and have not done this. I do not have this within me; I am not that man. Lord, please forgive me." You may also think of other people, and confess for them too. Or, you may say to God: "Lord, I am totally unable. I look to You, for this day You have laid this matter upon my heart." If God commands you to be an honest man, then you look to Him to make you an honest man. If He commands you to be a loving person, then you look to Him to make you a loving person.

By reading the commandment of God in this way, you perhaps will discover one thing, which is, that God's *commandment* is also God's *promise*. Whatever He commands, He without fail will give you the power t keep His commandment. If you see the commandment of God but imagine that He is troubling you by asking you to do what you cannot possibly do, then this is because you have not seen that God's command is always paired with promise.

Recall, if you will, the story of the rich young ruler recorded in Luke 18. After he had heard the Lord Jesus say to him, "One think thou lackest yet: sell all that thou hast, and distribute unto the poor, and thou shalt have treasure in heaven: and come, follow me" (v. 22), the young man went away sorrowfully. He felt he could keep all the Ten Commandments but *this* thing he could not do. The command of the Lord was too hard. Yet, the Lord later revealed that His command was not only command but also promise: "The things which are impossible with men are possible with God" (v. 27). Thank the Lord, His command always manifests two things: one is, that it is impossible with men; the other is, that it is possible with God. Therefore, whenever you are confronted with the commandment of God, do see on the one hand *your impossibility* but on the other hand *God's possibility.* Were you to see only your impossibility, you would plunge into sorrow; but if you can also see God's possibility, you will break out in praise.

How frequently in reading God's word you find that His command is beyond your ability. So you should pray, "Lord, *I* cannot; but, Lord, I thank You because *You* can. This is impossible with men, therefore it is impossible with me. But with You, all things are possible. So, I trust You to fulfill this in me." And thus shall you see how God will answer your prayer.

By learning to read God's word through reading and praying, we gradually touch the spirit of the word. We become aware of the great distance which exists between our personal condition and the spirit of God's word.

Take, for instance, the passage in Philippians 3. 18-19, which reads: "For many walk, of whom I told you often, and now tell you even weeping, that they are the enemies of the cross of Christ: whose end is perdition, whose god is the belly, and whose glory is in their shame, who mind earthly things." We may quite easily and correctly say that these are the enemies of God, whose end is perdition, but we have hardly touched the spirit of the writer of this Scripture passage. If we were to read through quickly, we would fail to touch the spirit of the writer. But if we were to pray and read at the same time—if we were to put ourselves in the place and the heart of the writer—we would readily see how full of love is his heart.

Let us see that one who was full of love was here being used by God to pronounce a very severe word. Let us see how he said it: "now I tell you even weeping." These people about whom Paul was writing had the belly as their god; they were the very enemies of the cross of Christ, and their end was perdition. All these were facts which he could not help but assert. Nevertheless, when Paul declared them, he was full of loving affection. It is relatively easy for us to learn to speak severely, but it is quite difficult to have such a loving spirit as Paul exhibited here. On the other hand, it is also simple and rather easy for some of us to be good-natured and always speak kindly of others, but it becomes impossible for us to ever say severe words such as Paul said here.

As we read this Scripture and actually touch the spirit of the writer, we will come to know *ourselves* as well as know the author. But if we do not touch the inner spirit as we read the word of God, it will leave us empty. Yet by reading and praying, our heart becomes single towards God, our spirit is opened to Him, and we shall be able to touch what is beyond the word. And thus shall we never feel dry, but instead be satisfied with living bread. In short, we shall be fed as we read.

We hope brothers and sisters will be attentive to read the word of God carefully each morning. Do not rush but read deliberately. Read and pray, pray and read. By reading each morning for but fifteen minutes, half an hour, or an hour, you will be fed and strengthened. You will have taken in God's word, and by so doing you shall experience the strength of the Lord throughout the day.

Four

Aside from reading the Bible in the early morn, you should spend some *other* time in reading the Bible. The Bible must be read systematically, frequently, and carefully. Then the word of Christ shall dwell in you richly.

Apart from personal reading, it is good when some brothers and sisters are together to sit down and read a portion of the Scriptures. It is highly profitable for the saints to memorize the Bible together. You yourself may not understand a certain verse, but strangely, as it is recited by another in your presence, you suddenly comprehend it. This is a fact. For light which is not available to an individual will be given in the assembling of the saints. Accordingly, it is better for brothers and sisters to open the Bible and read together, instead of saying idle words. Explanation of the word is not that important. One person may read while the rest listen, or all may read by turn. One may read the chapter he has read today, and another may read his chapter of the day. Through such reading you may learn a great deal in the Bible.

Reading the Bible is imperative for a Christian to do. Young brothers and sisters must cultivate at once this habit of reading the word in the early morning. We believe such reading is most profitable to spiritual progress. For such reading enables us to see the power of God's word. Some believers may have starved for a long duration—not just a few days, or for even a month, but perhaps for many years. Some people may have never fed upon the word of God in the early morning ever since they first became Christians. No wonder they are so weak! Oh! do let us feed upon the word of God. To read the Bible and pray in the morning is truly feeding on God's word. May the Lord deliver us from spiritual poverty, from poverty in His word. Let the word of Christ dwell in us richly that daily we may have life supplied us from His word.

G. WONDROUS THINGS ARE NATURALLY DONE

These signs shall accompany them that believe: in my name shall they cast out demons; they shall speak with

new tongues; they shall take up serpents, and if they drink
any deadly thing, it shall in no wise hurt them; they shall
lay hands on the sick, and they shall recover. (Mark 16.
17–18)

Blessed be Jehovah God, the God of Israel, who only
doeth wondrous things. (Ps. 72. 18)

Mark 16. 17–18 are words spoken by our Lord to
His eleven disciples. They speak of their doing wondrous things. How do we look at these things today?

One

One thing we need to be reminded of, and that is,
nothing in God's word is for performance and none
can perform it. Not only the words of Mark 16. 17–18
are not open to man's performance; *all* the words of
God are not subject to human acting. God is willing
to hear the prayer of Elijah on Mount Carmel and send
down fire to prove that Jehovah alone is God, and not
Baal (see 1 Kings 18. 30–39). Indeed, God will work
wonders to prove himself to be God, but He will not
allow any man to work wonders for the sake of performance. Some people think of using these two verses
in Mark 16 to validate their performance, but God will
turn away from them and let them fail. You cannot ac-
cuse such people of not believing in the words of Mark
16, for they *do* believe; yet God will not support their
claim nor defend their supposed integrity. For God is
God. He will only do what *He* wants to do; He will
not act according to man's idea.

Two

Let us well remember one spiritual principle: that faith is most natural and effortless. Some Christians do not understand much about faith, so having their prayers answered seems to require much labor. Each time they try to obtain God's answer, they have to apply such a heavy dose of faith that they almost cry out, "I am here believing! I am here believing!" Although their prayers may be heard, they have believed to the point of exhaustion. After having enough experience and having learned more, they pray, they believe, and God hears them, but they now have no need to exert so much effort as before. They will pray quite naturally, and God will answer them quite naturally. Formerly, their faith was so forced that it nearly broke their heart. They wanted to believe but they could not believe. They believed till they were exhausted in their faith. Now their faith is something very natural; it is spontaneous faith.

Three

Faith is spontaneous, and wondrous works are natural. No one who works wonders fancies he is working wonders. To the one who truly believes in God, wondrous works are quite common. Only those who are far away from God deem them extraordinary. All who live before God and close to Him consider wondrous works to be something ordinary.

At one time or another we must have all read the story of the children of Israel crossing the Red Sea. The first time we read it, we must have been amazed at the multitudes of people who crossed the Red Sea. Yet the Bible never recorded anything like shoutings by the people on this side of the Red Sea, saying, "How marvelous, the waters are divided!" or "Look, what a wonder this is!" No, they simply composed a song and sang only after they landed on the other side of the Sea. As they looked back, they realized what a great wonder it was. It is the same with the believers today. When the Lord works wonders in their lives, they have no idea that these *are* wondrous works. Only when they look back do they comprehend the greatness of God's works.

Recall, if you will, how many times God has healed your sickness. At those times, did you really think great things had happened? Many times you have encountered problems which were solved through God's grace, but at those moments did you understand God as working wonders? No, not until you looked back did you realize what great things had happened. Even this looking back is natural, and not deliberate.

Some people, viewing these verses from the human side, misconclude the words in Mark 16. 17–18 to signify the things mentioned there to be quite extraordinary. Yet as we think upon God, we will not at all be surprised. Compared to the crossing of the Red Sea by the children of Israel these other things in Mark are quite insignificant. The words in Mark do not mean that a believer can drink deadly things every day without dying. No, if anyone should drink deadly things deliberately, he will surely die. On the contrary, the Mark passage simply suggests our knowing God and His power: we acknowledge that there is nothing He cannot do. For wonders do not come by believing with great effort; they are the manifestations of God's mighty power. He is the God who works wonders. Whenever *He* works, wonders are performed. And furthermore, you and I will have no sense that doing wondrous works is difficult at all. The problem today lies in viewing these wonders from a great distance divorced from a true consideration of God. And thus wonders, within that kind of context, cannot help but become something very extraordinary. To those who are near to God, however, wonders are something quite commonplace in the house of God.

Formerly there was a girl who lived by the seashore, since her family fished for their living. Later on, she got married to a man who lived in the mountain. Life on the mountain was very hard. Due to inconvenience in transportation, daily commodities were rare. One day her father-in-law was very angry at her, saying, "This daughter-in-law knows nothing about frugality. She is truly a great spendthrift. For she consumed a crab in three days." He angrily went to her family in order to complain. While he was there, he was asked to eat with them. On the table were many crabs. Later he found in their yard piles of crab shells. He swallowed his complaint and returned home.

Many believers look upon wonders in the same fashion as that gentleman of the mountain looked upon crabs. They may experience some wondrous work only once in ten years, or even only once in thirty. No wonder they consider wonders to be extraordinary. But to those who truly live close before God, wonders are very common phenomena. The hand of God is the source of all wondrous works, and He is always working wonders.

Four

Hence wonders do not require our effort. Wonders happen when the power of God is manifested in our lives. Paul was once bitten by a viper but he simply "shook it off into the fire" and "took no harm" (see Acts 28. 3–5). Watch how this wonder worked that day in Paul's life. He had not said to the islanders of Melita, "Come, I am going to peform a wonder for you to see." He blew no trumpet but simply shook off the creature into the fire. Those who do not know God glory in the wondrous works, but those who truly know Him never boast of them. (Of course, this does not mean that all who do not magnify wonders know God. For some of them do not believe in Him, and therefore they cannot believe in wonders.) In fact, those who know God will never brag of wondrous works simply because wonders are quite natural to them.

Let me ask you: when your prayer is answered, do you feel you have done a marvelous thing. If so, this proves that your faith is yet immature. Were you truly to believe in the power of God, you would receive the answer to prayer unconsciously. Without knowing it, it would simply have been a case in which God had performed a wonder for you. Under such circumstances, wondrous works are natural, most effortless and common.

Let us always remember that wonders are something done unconsciously. If we are conscious about performing wonders, they will not come forth. In other words, when we decide to work wonders, these very things distance themselves from us. It is almost as if it were a case of: "to will is present with me, but to do that which is good is not" (Rom. 7. 18). However, as we live before God and believe in Him, wonders will happen unconsciously—just like Paul, who on the occasion already mentioned, quite unconsciously performed the wonder of not being hurt by a viper. He could not repeat the act were it to be publicly requested; nor could we imitate Paul under the impulse of people's persuasion. We can neither imitate others nor repeat ourselves. Here we touch one of the important principles in Christian experience; that is to say, God hearing prayers and doing wonders in our experience is something most natural and unpretentious. In the early days of our Christian walk, we might reckon ourselves as having great strength and unbelievable faith; yet as we progress in our walk and learn more, we will sense them no longer. We are not even aware of how we believe, but in simply committing ourselves to God, wonderful things are done.

Five

Many signs and wonders occurred in Paul's life, yet he confessed himself to be "in weakness, and in fear, and in much trembling" (1 Cor. 2. 3). God is willing to work through men, but He will not work through one who thinks he is able. People who do not know God proclaim that some particular person is able to do this or that wonder. Yet the one who truly knows God will concede that he does not know he is able. The person who is really used of God does not sense he can. What is done is done, that is all. Thank God, He is so powerful that He does everything without the need of us. The longer we are Christians, the simpler we should become. Whoever grows more complicated is being sidetracked. The more we know God, the simpler we are. Even believing becomes effortless. As we live before the Lord, we become simpler day by day. From the bottom of our hearts we shall readily acknowledge: "It is God, not we." If we truly know the Lord, His works in our lives will be most natural.

TITLES YOU
WILL WANT TO HAVE

by Watchman Nee

Basic Lesson Series
Volume 1—A Living Sacrifice
Volume 2—The Good Confession
Volume 3—Assembling Together
Volume 4—Not I, But Christ
Volume 5—Do All to the Glory of God
Volume 6—Love One Another

The Church and the Work
Volume 1—Assembly Life
Volume 2—Rethinking the Work
Volume 3—Church Affairs

The Spirit of the Gospel
The Life That Wins
From Glory to Glory
The Spirit of Judgment
From Faith to Faith
The Lord My Portion
Aids to "Revelation"
Grace for Grace
The Better Covenant
A Balanced Christian Life
The Mystery of Creation
The Messenger of the Cross
Full of Grace and Truth—Volume 1
Full of Grace and Truth—Volume 2
The Spirit of Wisdom and Revelation
Whom Shall I Send?
The Testimony of God
The Salvation of the Soul
The King and the Kingdom of Heaven
The Body of Christ: A Reality
Let Us Pray
God's Plan and the Overcomers
The Glory of His Life
"Come, Lord Jesus"
Practical Issues of This Life
Gospel Dialogue
God's Work
Ye Search the Scriptures
The Prayer Ministry of the Church
Christ the Sum of All Spiritual Things
Spiritual Knowledge
The Latent Power of the Soul
Spiritual Authority
The Ministry of God's Word
Spiritual Reality or Obsession
The Spiritual Man

by Stephen Kaung

Discipled to Christ
The Splendor of His Ways
Seeing the Lord's End in Job
The Songs of Degrees
Meditations on Fifteen Psalms

ORDER FROM:

Christian Fellowship Publishers, Inc.
11515 Allecingie Parkway
Richmond, Virginia 23235